SELFONOM

*How Broadly-defined
Self-interest Explains
Everything!*

memememememememememememememememememememe
memememememememememememememememememememe
memememememememememememememememememememe
memememememememememememememememememememe
memememememememememememememememememememe
memememememememememememememememememememe
memememememememememememememememememememe
memememememememememememememememememememe
memememememememememememememememememememe
memememememememememememememememememememe
memememememememememememememememememememe
memememememememememememememememememememe

ANTHONY J. GRIBIN, PH.D.

Cover design by Anthony J. Gribin

ISBN 978-0-9827376-4-4

First Edition

TTGpress

To Jack Gribin, who taught me how to think

Acknowledgments:

HD
DBF
JL

CONTENTS

CHAPTER 4: WHY DON'T WE TALK ABOUT SELF-INTEREST?

Being thought of as "out for oneself" is not very flattering so we don't talk about it. Even though it dominates our everyday lives and is eminently human, we just can't, don't or won't see ourselves that way. Self-interest is easily rationalized, as are other difficult to discuss topics such as racism and sexual history.

PART II: SELFONOMICS IN EVERYDAY LIFE

CHAPTER 5: SELF-INTEREST THROUGH THE LIFE CYCLE

Rules, customs and limits, taught to us by parents and teachers, help us to channel, restrain and guide our SI as we progress from childhood, through the teenage years, to adulthood, with revisions being made throughout.

CHAPTER 6: SELF-INTEREST AT THE FAMILY LEVEL

The expenses of a middle-class family are examined, to see how much of what they earn goes to fulfill self-interest of one kind or another.

CHAPTER 7: SELF-INTEREST FROM A PSYCHOLOGIST'S POINT OF VIEW

Non-biologically-based mental health issues, addictions and self-defeating behaviors are examined in patients, using the various subcategories of SI.

CHAPTER 12: THE AMERICAN DREAM

The desire to "get ahead," to provide for one's family, to build a nest egg and to save for retirement is examined in the lives of average Americans. In fallow times, this "pursuit of happiness" can lead us to financial ruin. The problem reverts back to the rules and laws within which self-interest is allowed to operate.

PART IV: FROM "WE THE PEOPLE" TO "ME THE PEOPLE"

CHAPTER 13: GREED

Upon examination, wealthy people have not cornered the market on greed. This leads to the hypothesis that all people act in their own self-interest, all the time, in every arena. Will it hold water?

CHAPTER 14: POLITICAL SELF-INTEREST

Just as our forebears intended us to chase the American Dream, they also directed us to vote our self-interest. Most political issues are matters of opinion, which opens us to bias and intentionally misleading information, making fact-checking essential.

CHAPTER 15: SELF-INTEREST AND RELIGION

What can explain the universality of religion is not necessarily the existence of God, but the certainty of human mortality. A parable is given to explain the belief in a supreme being, based on the human need for comfort in the face of death. Selfonomics can account for organized religion, as well as the eminence of religious leaders, whether or not God exists.

Chapter 16: Problems Created by Technology

Though technology can empower self-interest, this can be used for good or for evil. Technology has been used recently to hide peoples' financial agendas, to bias and exaggerate information, and to foment holy war. Since technology advances so rapidly, many of its effects are not yet knowable.

Chapter 17: Competing Self-Interests and "Entitlements"

Attempts to reduce the national deficit has focused attention on entitlement programs, such as Medicare and Medicaid. The self-interest of patients, physicians, nurses and attorneys are highly correlated, and works against trimming costs. An NPR interview with physicians illustrates how self-interest and the absence of discussion about it, affects decisions about health care.

Part V: Solutions

Chapter 18: The Alignment of Self-Interests

Non-alignment of self-interest between friends can be handled by time apart. Between spouses, vastly differing self-interests will result in unhappiness on one or both parts and possible dissolution of the relationship if compromises cannot be found.

CHAPTER 19: COLLECTIVE SELF-INTEREST

Collective SI is defined as what is good for our planet and its living inhabitants. ISI can work against, be neutral to, or support CSI. Ten Principles for helping ISI to correlate highly with CSI are suggested.

CHAPTER 20: LESSONS LEARNED

It is concluded that self-interest, all the time, fits the data from the range of human behavior in all realms, including altruism, religion, everyday life, psychological problems, as well as economics and politics. An analogy is made between the inevitability of water flowing down a river and the natural existence of self-interest in humans. In a stream, the only way to change the course of the water is to create a dam or dike; with self-interest, it can only be channeled through rules and laws. Suggestions for changes are made, including the need for new professions of "Self-Interest Predictors" and "Fact Checkers."

INTRODUCTION

I've been thinking about the material in this book, which involves a trail leading from psychology to economics and politics, for years. Usually I can focus on one issue, say the relationship between self-interest and the life cycle, or politics, and stay on task. Occasionally, circumstances allow, or maybe create, a time in which there is a juxtaposition of seemingly unrelated topics. This happened after a recent surgery which for me, led from thinking about abject pain, to word play on a book title, to the similarity between what happens in psychotherapy and behavioral economics. Go figure.

I'm quite grateful that the pain phase didn't last too long. But having nothing to do but move a leg an inch, one way or the other, did give me time to think. The pain connected me to a book called "Predictably Irrational" by Dan Ariely,[1] who described insights gleaned while spending three years in hospital recovering from a horrible accident. The follow-on connection then took me to the works of Steven Levitt and Stephen Dubner, authors of "Freakonomics"[2] and "Superfreakonomics."[3] These three men are behavioral economists, whose work I admire fully.

There has always been a divergence of opinion in economics about whether humans behave rationally all of the time or just most of the time. Classical economists, such as Adam Smith posited the former in the 1700s in

[1] Ariely, D. (2008). *Predictably Irrational.* HarperCollins.

[2] Levitt, S. & Dubner, S.J. (2005). *Freakonomics: A Rogue Economist Explores the Hidden Side of Everything.* William Morrow/HarperCollins.

[3] Levitt, S. & Dubner, S.J. (2009). *Superfreakonomics: Global Cooling, Patriotic Prostitutes, and Why Suicide Bombers Should Buy Life Insurance.* William Morrow/HarperCollins, 2009.

"The Theory of Moral Sentiments," and John Stuart Mill coined the term "homo economicus" to imply that men were rational actors in their own self-interest. The observations, however, of some Neoclassical economists, that humans often make decisions that don't make sense in terms of costs and rewards, imply that humans are driven to choices by their emotions and can therefore be seen as irrational.[4]

My own experiences as a long-time therapist have led me to believe that people are, in fact, rational. (My reasoning will come later.) Instead of Ariely's assertion, that humans are "predictably irrational," I have come to see them as "unpredictably rational." That is, people always express good reasons for doing what they did, but because I wasn't in their head, I couldn't see those reasons. Changing the language slightly, I observed the conclusions of logical processes, in the form of behaviors in my patients, but had no idea of the premises that went into deducing those conclusions. Once those premises were revealed and discussed, the behaviors of patients seemed eminently rational. I add the modifier "unpredictably" to both align myself with Ariely's word usage and to indicate that I don't know all of the premises of any one patient at any one time, although with repeated contact the hit rate gets better.

As for Levitt and Dubner, they advertise that their books (and wonderful blog) offer "The Hidden Side of Everything." Their analysis of the reasons for the decline in teenage crime in the 1990s ("Freakonomics") is fascinating, as is their deconstruction of the famous Kitty Genovese murder case of the early 1960s ("Superfreakonomics"). They are expert analysts and compelling story-tellers. It turns out though, again from my point of view, is that what

---

[4] The concept of "bounded rationality," for example, asserts that man's rationality is limited by his knowledge, his ability and the time he has to make a decision. See Simon, Herbert. (1957) Models of Man, Social and Rational: Mathematical Essays on Rational Human Behavior in a Social Setting. New York: Wiley.

they are looking to explain is unusual behavior or unusual linkage between seemingly disparate behaviors, which is very similar to what I do in therapy. And their entertaining and frequent counterintuitive findings come down to unearthing a group of (previously unknown) premises on which people act, that produces those behaviors. Steven D. Levitt echoed this supposition in a recent blog[5], "When I see a mistake as egregious as this [referring to an estimate of the cost per car sold of the 2009 "Cash for Clunkers" program], I usually suspect it is more likely the result of someone trying to intentionally deceive the public rather than an error of logic. So the first thing I do is try to figure out the incentives of the group that is making the statement."

Levitt used the word "incentives." In therapy, I see "incentives" under every rock, behind every tree and in every patient. Except that I've come to use the term "self-interest." Patients seem to be looking out for themselves, or think they are, even though many do it in quite ass backwards or misguided ways. Some make themselves "happy" by using drugs or cheating on their partners, others "protect" themselves by becoming reclusive to avoid rejection.

As I became more interested in events in the political and economics spheres, it was clear that self-interest follows patterns identical to what I see in therapy. Not only that, but self-interest seems to be a constant, ubiquitous, rampant and increasingly obvious force in our world. Though this is a very strong statement, I believe that self-interest has become a force that threatens American society as we know it. Or knew it.

Why do I say this? At the risk of telegraphing some of my punches, I'll explain. There is a confluence of discomfiting trends. First, our world is getting a lot more

---

[5] Freakonomics Blog, November 4, 2009.

complicated. And the complexity seems to be accelerating. Think of Moore's law, which posits that computing speed and memory size doubles approximately every two years. Although this may be an exaggeration of the rate of growth of our sources of information, compare the state of media that existed thirty years ago, to that which is extant today. Back then there were three main networks, one or two local newspapers which provided most of our news, and one local news radio station. Today there are many more networks, thousands of news-pushing websites and blogs, each presenting the "truth" with a capital "T." Information now competes for our time and attention with easily available music and videos on iPads, social networks such as Facebook and Twitter, as well as computer games and email. Our sources of input are diluted as our experiences become more individual and unique.

As people spend more time in diversionary media, they have less time to get information, especially reliable information. There are few reliable facts any more. If something is presented to us as "a fact," we don't know if it is accurate or not. We don't have time to do "due diligence" on what we hear. It is easier to subscribe to "truthiness,"[6] believing what we want to believe, and seeking out sources of information that support what we believed to begin with. "Confimation bias" is rampant, which is both a cause and effect of attitude polarization.[7]

---

[6] Truthiness: Merriam-Webster's #1 word of the year for 2006.
1.   "truth that comes from the gut, not books" (Stephen Colbert, Comedy Central's "The Colbert Report," October 2005)
2.   "the quality of preferring concepts or facts one wishes to be true, rather than concepts or facts known to be true" (American Dialect Society, January 2006)

[7] See the Wikipedia article on "confirmation bias" for a summary.

What these trends have increasingly produced is a preponderance of low-information voters,[8] ones that can be easily swayed into voting for someone else's self-interest, rather than their own. We get our information more through the rumor mills of Facebook, Twitter and the break room where we work, than through legitimate sources. And the less we know, the more we turn to a leader, religious or political, to guide us.

Both religious and political figures have a vested (self-)interest in staying in power, so a charismatic leader who is light on substance can sway large numbers of people by bending facts.[9] Often this type of leader is anti-science because science is not open to distortion and is apolitical. A charismatic leader like this can assert that evolution is just "a theory," and/or can deny the existence of global climate change in the face of overwhelming scientific evidence. Or can spout non-specific calls to arms that are very hard to disagree with without appearing unpatriotic or being accused of being a "communist." "Let's put America first!" or "It's time we stopped arguing and started putting Americans back to work!" or "We can't let the Chinese outproduce Americans!" mean little but are effective in raising adrenaline levels in some listeners. As Maureen Dowd noted, "The occupational hazard of democracy is know-nothing voters. It shouldn't be know-nothing candidates."

---

[8] "A low-information voter is the euphemistic term for a person who votes with very little (if any) knowledge of who or what they are voting for. It might also describe someone who votes for a person for trivial reasons (i.e., 'I'd like to have a beer with him!' or 'She just seems so nice!'). They are the voters who don't pay attention, don't research races and are relatively open to manipulation by 30-second commercials or 5-second sound bites." Spokane Skeptic. "The Low-Information Voter." August 31, 2009. http://spokaneskeptic.blogspot.com/2009/08/low-information-voters.html

[9] Or dismissing science, since "facts have a liberal bias." I believe this was first stated by Paul Krugman.

Among low-information voters, the style of a politician is often more important than substance. Witness Sarah Palin, whose looks and charismatic delivery made her a rock star among conservatives. Rick Perry may have been her male equivalent in the 2012 Presidential race. What people get out of following this type of candidate may be a vicarious connection to someone glamorous, someone who seems to care about what is important to them (or says he/she does), and who makes them feel like they're part of a team. Without this appeal, it is difficult to understand how people who are not affluent and are not deeply invested in social issues (abortion, gay rights, religiosity) would vote for a Conservative candidate who believes in a trickle down approach to the economy.[10] It's just plainly against their self-interest.

A second factor is that the income gap is widening. The rich are getting richer while the poor are barely holding their own if they are fortunate, or are losing their jobs to the recession and their homes to foreclosure if they are not. The wealthy believe in trickle down economics which seems to just make the situation worse. The argument of the affluent is that helping "small businesses" creates jobs. The facts don't support this assertion. So now, Wall St. executives, financial nabobs, large corporations and stockholders are doing well despite a terrible recession still in our rear view mirror. Yet as of early 2014, there have been recent cuts to food stamp programs at the same time

---

[10] Which liberal (and well-respected) economists strenuously argue doesn't work. If trickle down worked, they say, it would've already done so considering that the Bush tax cuts for the wealthy, the availability of cheap money (10 year T-Bill at 2% as of September, 2011) and loopholes in the tax laws that allow many large corporations to pay little or no corporate taxes, have put plenty of money in the hands of the wealthy. See Reich, Robert. "The Zero Economy." Truthout, September 4, 2011 and Reich's blog: http://robertreich.org/post/9709926186. Also Krugman, Paul. "The Fatal Distraction." New York Times Op-Ed, September 4. 2011.

that the stock market is at record highs. Apparently, the poor have too much to eat.

In effect, we are taking from the bottom of society, which doesn't have a lot to give, and handing wealth to the top economic strata. It is not direct or intentional; that is, the wealthy are not stealing money from their poorer brethren directly. But through the last few years of painful unemployment and home foreclosure, it is the less fortunate who are inordinately affected. The wealthy use their power to further their own self-interest and are usually successful at it. There are very few people who start out wealthy who end up abjectly poor. For a middle class person, all it takes to go into poverty is the loss of a job, since re-finding employment is next to impossible in 2011. And if you are not young, are a minority, are not good looking, it's even worse.

Third, technology has also allowed the potentiation of the self-interest of all of us, which can be used for good or evil. As an example, the rich have more and more money to spend on swaying elections. The Citizens United decision by the Supreme Court allows corporations to give as much as they want to any candidate. Since corporations are usually on the same side as the wealthy and the conservative side of the populace, this creates inequalities and the prospect of perpetuating those inequalities. To be fair, progressives have their rich donors also, not that it makes the situation better.

The combination of these factors, i.e. an increasingly complex world, the widening income gap between rich and poor, and the growing power of technology, makes it easy to misrepresent of make up the "truth."   Especially when the messages are delivered to low-information voters. Candidates can bend numbers to their advantage and no one calls them on it ("truthiness" and "proofiness"[11]). Bright

---

[11] Seife, Charles. (2010). Proofiness: The Dark Arts of Mathematical Deception. Viking.

people who can't or don't take the time to check facts, often find it easier to jump on the bandwagon of ignorance and support positions that are bereft of substance but are delivered with plenty of style.

Where are these changes going to take us, as a society? Theoretically, if the income disparity gets much worse, we might be inviting revolt down the road against an increasingly powerful upper class. The "Occupy movement," which began in New York may be a progenitor. Short of that, however, our Constitution is being sorely tested to keep our country stable. Consider these recent occurrences:

1) The Citizens United decision by the Supreme Court, guided by their interpretation of our Constitution, allows corporations to be treated as individual citizens and give unlimited donations to political campaigns with very little transparency. Elections can be swayed by the oligarchs, if not bought. It should be obvious that money can buy power and power can make someone wealthier. It is a terrible spiral. And on April 2, 2014 SCOTUS passed a party line decision to remove limits from how much an individual can give to any one candidate.[12]

2) The *perfectly legal* negotiating tactic of refusal that has recently been utilized by Republicans in the House of

---

[12] This author's comment, published in the New York Times on that day (no big deal) stated, "Suppose I have an extra hundred million lying around. I go to states that have contested races for Senate and the House. I walk around and ask people who they will vote for. If my team is A, and they say "B," I offer them a contract saying "If A wins, I will give you a $1000. If B wins, you get nothing." A hundred million would buy at minimum 100,000 votes. But many more would switch. Joe goes to three friends and says, "Hey guys, if A wins I'll give you a hundred bucks. If he doesn't, you lose nothing." Another nice part is that on the off chance that B wins, I don't have to pay out! How many races can I buy??? Notice that I'm not really buying anyone's vote, but I'm aligning their self-interests with my own."

Representatives to effectively block legislation unless the other side capitulates to their demands. Less kindly, the strategy has been called "hostage taking of the U.S. and global economies" and "political terrorism."[13] In December of 2011 House Republicans refused to continue Bush era tax cuts for the middle class unless they were extended for the wealthy as well. Obama gave in, but was warned by Paul Krugman of the New York Times, among others, that the blackmail would not stop there. More recently, House Republicans refused to vote for any deficit reduction program that included increased taxes. This relatively new, but apparently effective strategy does not bode well for our democratic process.

3) The Senate, which has (as of early 2010) 59 Democrats representing 62.7% of the population[14] is blocked from passing bills by 41 Republicans representing 37.3% of the people. This belies the notion of rule by the majority, or even supermajority which is pegged at 60%.

4) Playing by the rules set by our body of laws no longer assures success. Getting adjustable rate mortgages was totally legal in 2008. Both lenders and borrowers played by the rules, but when the economy went into recession, both suffered. A new class of poor people was created when many lost their houses, their jobs and their assets. As society becomes more complex, the issues and rules dealing with those issues become more complex, and the opportunity for things to go awry increases due to unintended and/or unforeseen consequences. Again, nothing illegal.

5) One of our two major political parties, the Republicans, has made it standard practice for candidates to

---

[13] Lofgren, Mike. "Goodbye to All That: Reflections of a GOP Operative Who Left the Cult." Truthout, September 3, 2011.

[14] How this number was arrived at appears later in the book.

demonstrate their religious bona fides in order to run for office. "...if the American people poll more like Iranians or Nigerians than Europeans or Canadians on questions of evolution versus creationism, scriptural inerrancy, the existence of angels and demons, and so forth, that result is due to the rise of the religious right, its insertion into the public sphere by the Republican Party and the consequent normalizing of formerly reactionary or quaint beliefs."[15] So much for the separation of Church and State.

6) The Constitution is a remarkable document considering that it was devised by people that lived in a primitive society by our standards. It is yet to be determined whether it can handle challenges posed by technology on steroids, such as the fomentation of terrorism, gambling, pornography and economic trade, especially because all of these involve global problems which know no national borders.

7) The Constitution says that we are all created equal. Unfortunately, after birth, many of us are just plain screwed (pardon the language). With the wealth gap increasing, a large part of our society will never catch up. And with the wealth gap, comes an information and technology gap, an education gap, a power gap and a health gap. The humane goal of feeding our population, putting a roof over their heads and allowing them access to healthcare seems to be getting further and further away.[16]

---

[15] Lofgren, op.cit.

[16] See Krugman, Paul. "Free To Die." New York Times Op-Ed, September 15, 2011. "In the past, conservatives accepted the need for a government-provided safety net on humanitarian grounds. Don't take it from me, take it from Friedrich Hayek, the conservative intellectual hero, who specifically declared in 'The Road to Serfdom' his support for 'a comprehensive system of social insurance' to protect citizens against 'the common hazards of life,' and singled out health in particular." He points out that the lack of compassion, especially among Conservatives goes directly against Hayek's beliefs.

Our country is not coming apart at the seams. At least not yet. But politics seem to be more divisive and partisan than ever before and is allowing the self-interests of small numbers of people to capture, control and override the self-interests of the majority. The problem invariably devolves back to the nature of self-interest itself.[17]

Why self-interest? Through the millennia self-interest was and is the key to survival for both ourselves and our progeny. It has been finely honed into us, in a Darwinian sense. And not merely the self-interest that leads us to go after what we want, but also the self-interest that protects us from whatever dangers lurk in the world around us, be they saber-tooth tigers or modern day hucksters. Self-interest is the font of competition and the basis of our capitalistic society. But just as we depend on self-interest to survive and flourish, we may be carrying around the seeds of our own destruction.

Thousands of years ago, there was enough land for your tribe and mine. Beating each other up over land didn't make much sense. These days, however, many more things are zero-sum. If you get x, that means I can't have x. If your taxes decrease, mine increase. If the government spends money on your town, there is less money for projects in mine. Live and let live works as long as letting live has a better cost-reward outcome than not letting live. When there is competition for resources such as oil or land or food, letting live may not be quite as appealing. And, as technology improves, the cost of me hurting more people at greater range becomes less, and at diminished consequence to my own interests.

If our political system is constructed around voting our self-interest and our economic system is born out of

---

[17] "Stable societies are breeding grounds for interest groups. Over time, these interest groups use government to establish sinecures for themselves, which gradually strangle the economy they are built on - like parasitic vines around a tree." Brooks, David. "The Vigorous Virtues." New York Times Op-Ed September 1, 2011.

competition for resources, and our biology is guided by "survival of the fittest," how can self-interest NOT be the cardinal, central trait of our existence? How can we NOT look out for ourselves psychologically and socially? The reader might be thinking that surely there are exceptions, but we may find out that these "buts" disappear in self-interest that is subtle, masked and denied. Ironically, for some of us, at certain times, self-interest can create "good" in the world.

What all this leads to is a need to carefully study the self-interests of people, groups and nations to see what we can learn about what is happening to us as a species and, more importantly what, if anything, we can do about it. This study is called "Selfonomics." The rest of this book is dedicated to this goal, beginning with very basic forms of self-interest found in individuals and working up to more complex situations found in the economic and political spheres.

Part I: The Elephant in the Room

The phrase, "the elephant in the room" is idiomatic. It is an issue or problem that everyone knows about, but doesn't talk about because it is easier *not* to discuss. It is ignored because it causes embarrassment or humiliation, or is socially taboo (such as race, religion, abortion or suicide.) The issue may be emotionally charged, such as divorce or alcoholism, leading family members to be reluctant to discuss or eager to avoid discussion altogether. People pretend the "elephant" is not there and deal with less important subjects, although everyone knows that the "elephant" will not go away by itself. From my point of view, the elephant in everyone's room is self-interest.

CHAPTER ONE: DEFINING TERMS

You are driving your car on the highway. What do you see directly in front of you? The road? Lane dividers? Other cars? Perhaps rain? What about the glass that forms the windshield in front of you? Often we overlook things that are too close to us...

Self-interest is omnipresent. Consider the following questions:

What do naive people who fall for get-rich-quick schemes and lose all their money have in common with Wall Street executives? How can ultra-wealthy financiers accept more and more money, in the form of salary, bonuses and stock options, and how can mortgage brokers lend money to people that they know will have a difficult time paying back the money? (They all are feeding their self-interest by trying to make or get more money or wealth.)

Why do we never see ourselves as greedy, but have no trouble seeing someone else that way? Why is it easier to blame others than shoulder the blame ourselves. How, when two people argue, can both think they're right and both think the other person started it?

Why do we all try to protect our egos; and why do we all want or need to see ourselves as good people.—

What does the teenager who goes to a Friday night party, have in common with another teen, who chooses not to go to the same party? How is asking someone out on a date the same as not asking him or her out? (Each person is looking out for themselves, but in very different ways.)

Why does the Golden Rule, i.e. "Do unto others as you would have them do unto you..." appear, in one form or another, in every society, in every age? Why does religion, in one form or another, with different representations of supreme beings, appear in every culture, since the dawn of history? (Hint: Self-interest cannot exist unopposed else we'd kill each other. Religion, laws, governments all keep a lid on self-interest.)

Why are such obviously good goals as universal health care, dealing with global warming and achieving peace among nations, so difficult to work on? (The self-interest of some people is often the opposite of the self-interest of others.)

Self-interest underlies the behavior of the people and issues listed above. As stated, we often overlook things that are too close to us... Self-interest, broadly defined, is a constant factor in people's conscious or not conscious thoughts and behavior, and is an elephant in-every room that we just don't talk about.[18] As will become clear however, it is not the same self-interest that is posited by economists, but one that is gleaned by a psychologist from observing the way people actually behave.

What exactly is self-interest? Is it the same in every person? Are there differences in kind or by degree between people? To begin, let's look at the statements immediately below and think about what the people mentioned have in common with each other...

Mary watches a television show.
Little Larry takes a cookie from the cookie jar.
Bill plants tomatoes in his backyard.
Dan plays tennis with a friend.
Quentin buys food at the supermarket.

All five people are doing something that they want or need to do for themselves. Mary enjoys watching her show, Little Larry loves cookies, Bill looks forward to eating his tomatoes, Dan enjoys the exercise and camaraderie, and Quentin likes to, or at least needs to, eat. Each of these folks is doing something *directly* for themselves. They will feel better either performing the above respective activities while they are in the act, or after they have acted.

We'll define these types of behaviors as serving *direct* self-interest. **Direct self-interest (DSI) is doing something through assertion that makes you feel good, or better in the short or long run. It involves looking out for your own needs, likes or wants. It involves pleasure-seeking behavior.** Other examples of direct

---

[18] According to Frank Rich, "...the elephant in the room... ...would be big money - the big money that dominates our political system, regardless of who's in power. Two years after the economic meltdown, most Americans now recognize that that money has inexorably institutionalized a caste system where everyone remains (at best) mired in economic stasis except the very wealthiest sliver." From: "Still the Best Congress Money Can Buy." New York Times, November 27, 2010.

self-interest are choosing a restaurant, buying a shirt, playing a sport or game, making lots of money, or even writing a book. **Since each of these assertions involves only one person, we'll also call them acts of Individual Self-Interest (ISI).** The five actions above are both examples of DSI and ISI.

Let's move to a second set of actions, each involving two people. What do they all have in common?

John asks Lisa out, and she says "yes."
Phil asks Betty out and she says "no."
Al and Dave argue about politics.
Bob and Joyce agree on which movie to see on Saturday night.
Joe buys a new computer and Carol disagrees strongly with the purchase.

Again, all ten are somehow looking out for their own needs, likes or wants. John asks Lisa out because he "likes" her, and she says yes, perhaps because she "likes" him in return, or because she's bored and has nothing better to do, or maybe because she wants to show her ex-boyfriend that he's not the only fish in the sea. In any case, she *wants* to go.

Phil isn't so lucky. He likes Betty, and asserts himself, but she turns him down. She's looking out for *herself* as well. Maybe she doesn't reciprocate his feelings, or perhaps she's busy doing something else, but by declining, she's looking out for herself.

Al and Dave arguing allows each to stick up for their core beliefs, provides one or both the chance to play "devil's advocate" or is just an entertaining way to pass an afternoon. In any case, they must like doing it or it must serve some other purpose for them. Bob and Joyce both meet *their own* needs by agreeing on a movie, while Joe and Carol's needs seem to run in opposite directions.

All ten of these people are, as the first group of five were, looking out for their DSI. And since each makes their decisions as an individual, they are also exhibiting ISI as well, except two at a time. **Self-interest can be analyzed in an individual, in pairs of individuals or, as we'll see later, larger groups or even nations.** The next group of five seem to be different. How?

> Ralph doesn't ask a co-worker out because he's
>   afraid of being turned down.
> Johnny doesn't raise his hand in class because he's
>   shy.
> Vic goes to visits his parents to avoid feeling bad
>   about not going.
> Barbara gives in to her husband to avoid an
> argument.
> Nick tells a lie about homework to avoid being
> grounded.

This group of five is particularly important because it helps to separate the "rational self-interest" of economic thought and various theories of "egoism."[19]

These five are also serving their own needs, even if it seems to us (looking from the outside) that those needs are self-defeating and protective or perhaps just dead wrong. Ralph "likes" the co-worker, can be friendly to her in work situations, but gets cold feet, feeling that a turn-down is certain. So he *protects* his ego by not asking her out. Johnny has always been shy and avoids discomfort by not raising his hand and not making eye contact with his teacher. He prays not to be called on, and is relieved when the lesson is over.

Guilt was instilled in Vic over the years by his parents, and he goes to visit them mainly because if he doesn't go, his mother will berate him, or he will know that she *would* berate him, and he will feel bad. To avoid these

---

[19] More on this later.

bad feelings he goes over to their house. Barbara is married to an imperious man and often finds it easier to give in rather than to get into a disagreement that often ends in her being talked down to or yelled at. And Nick knows that if he tells the truth about his homework, he will not be allowed to hang out with his friends this weekend, so he lies about it, hoping not to get caught.

These five are also looking out for themselves, but not in a direct way. **Each gives more weight to avoiding negative consequences than to seeking positive ones.** They fear rejection (Ralph), humiliation (Johnny), guilt (Vic), confrontation (Barbara), and punishment (Nick). If one can place him or herself in the shoes of these five, avoiding rejection, ending a humiliating situation, reducing guilt, side-stepping confrontation and escaping punishment all *feel good or make a bad feeling go away.* They are looking out for themselves in an indirect, backwards or *protective* way. **We'll call this strategy, however beneficial or harmful it may be, Protective Self-Interest, or PSI.** PSI and DSI are very different, yet both serve an individual's self-interest. **DSI is pleasure-seeking, while PSI is pain-avoiding.** Both PSI and DSI are examples of ISI.

This second type of self-interest is crucial to the explanatory power of Selfonomics. Self-interest is a duality, PSI and DSI being two sides of the same coin. In the evolutionary process, it's not just how good a predator you are, it's also how well you avoid being preyed upon. In sports, it's not just how many points or runs or goals *you* score, it's how many you avoid being scored on *you.* It's offense *and* defense. In poker and other games (such as the lottery), it's not only how many times you win, but how many times you avoid losing (by staying in a hand with lousy cards, or buying too many lottery tickets).

Historically, one may ask why there is a variety of the "Golden Rule" in every culture through the ages. The answer is that there needs to be something to contain, curtail or preclude the pursuit of abject direct self-interest.

In effect, the Golden Rule provides a limit to self-interest; it represents protective self-interest. Laws, guidelines, procedures all serve to limit DSI.[20]

PSI is what allows us to account for what others have labeled "irrational behavior." In experiments reported on by Ariely in "Predictably Irrational,"[21] whenever a subject does not maximize monetary gain, the behavior is deemed irrational. In Selfonomics, maximizing monetary gain is Direct Self-Interest, which is only half of the story. When Protective Self-Interest is factored in (which in those experiments can be manifested in guilt, shame, social conformity, embarrassment or another negative emotion), the behaviors make sense. They are, however, less predi table because while DSI is easily measured in terms of monetary outcome, the avoided negative emotions are a lot more elusive, being harder to both scale and measure.

Consider the last set of five people:

> Fred buys a hot muscle car, overlooking its mechanical problems.
> Barbara drinks too many beers with her friends too often.
> Sally makes an impulse buy on her credit card.
> Rob cheats on his faithful girlfriend with a "hottie."
> Jen speeds in her car, thinking she won't get caught.

These five act in ways that they think support their needs, likes or wants, but at some later time, come to regret their decisions. All five are examples of DSI, because the actions are basically pleasure-seeking, yet their actions seem to us to be *misguided* in the sense that indicates poor judgment. We'll call these types **Misguided**

---

[20] In psychoanalysis, Freud's id represents DSI, the superego PSI, with the ego being the balancer between them. The rules and customs and limits we are taught by our parents serve as PSI to our natural DSI.

[21] op. cit.

Self-Interest, or MSI. Note that these examples are all DSI and ISI that are also MSI.

MSI is *not* a third category of self-interest; it is a way of evaluating the quality of people's actions and motivations. Someone who makes bad choices frequently (exhibits MSI often) will not have an easy life; someone who rarely exhibits MSI will have a smoother path.

To economists or politicians, MSI doesn't matter; they're just amassing statistics or analyzing voting patterns. But for a Psychologist, the pattern and extent of MSI can give a picture of the patient's modus operandi and may point out ways of helping them.

Misguided Self-Interest is almost always a value judgment and can often not be labeled until after the fact. If an adult smokes marijuana occasionally, opinions may differ as to whether this represents moderate DSI or DSI that is MSI. On the other hand, someone drinking to excess will be seen by most (but not all) as an example of MSI. People can disagree on what comprises MSI. Perceived MSI will vary with our beliefs, the frequency of the behavior and even the consequences received (as in getting a DWI).

Some behaviors can be PSI in the short run but MSI in the long run. If I give in to my partner to avoid an argument or I tell a lie to my parents about my grades to avoid punishment, my needs might be served in the short term, but result in long term habits that are certainly not good for me.

Of course many PSI actions are *not* MSI. Getting out of the house when it's on fire, fighting back in self-defense, leaving the scene of a bar fight and choosing conservative investments are all examples of PSI behaviors that are *not* misguided. Stopping your drinking after two beers and waiting a long time before getting behind the wheel also represents PSI that is not MSI.

Sometimes we cannot know if DSI, or the absence of PSI, is misguided or not. Take Don, who is twenty-two and just out of college. He's working two part-time jobs and is barely able to make ends meet. He has no health insurance, and feels he can't even afford an inexpensive policy that will cover a catastrophe without giving up small enjoyments such as beer and an occasional night out. He's healthy now, and if he stays that way, he will have gambled and won. If he breaks an arm playing football with his pals, he will have gambled and lost. Hindsight, and a $5,000 hospital bill will tell him, with perfect accuracy, that his self-interest was misguided. His decision to not sign up for health insurance works out if he stays healthy, but has serious financial consequences if anything untoward happens.

In a way, DSI without some concurrent PSI can result in trouble. If a person doesn't know when to stop drinking (or can't stop), or gets behind the wheel of a car after overdoing it, disaster may result. The phrase "too much of a good thing" fits here. Playing golf occasionally is not likely to anger your domestic partner; playing twice a week is. You have to know when to stop. That's PSI limiting DSI.

Too much PSI without some DSI can also be misguided. An extreme case is that of an agoraphobic, who only feels safe in his own house, but there are also less extreme examples of conservative and cautious behavior, that may put a damper on one's life if taken to extremes.   Miserliness (*always* saving for a rainy day) or never asking anyone out or always staying home to avoid rejection come to mind. The phrase "everything in moderation" fits here.

It is often difficult to know in advance whether or not protective self-interest is misguided. Take the case of a man or a woman staying in a loveless,emotionally abusive marriage for the sake of the children or out of a need for security. Is staying misguided or not? It's tough to know in advance. Probability dictates that if a man or woman is attractive, wealthy, doesn't have much baggage (kids, child support, alimony) and is gregarious, the odds are better that leaving may work out. On the other hand, someone with four bratty kids, the prospect of lots of child support or alimony, no money, who will become embittered might be better off staying put. Whether a decision is misguided or not can usually be assessed only after the fact and the pluses and minuses that enter into the decision are both confluential and complicated.

In sum:

> **Self-interest motivates all of us, all the time. It involves anything that makes us feel good, or helps us to feel less bad.**
>
> **Self-interest in an individual is called Individual Self-Interest, or ISI.**
>
> **Self-interest that involves assertively filling ones needs, makes one feel better, or involves pleasure seeking behavior is called Direct Self-Interest, or DSI.**
>
> **Self-interest that involves protection from, or avoidance of, negative feelings, real or imagined, is called Protective Self-Interest, or PSI.**
>
> **Self-interest that is direct or protective that results in unwanted consequences is called Misguided Self-Interest, or MSI. MSI can often only be assessed in hindsight, may serve DSI or PSI in the short run but not the long run, and depends on the assessor's beliefs.**
>
> **Finally, to describe the study of the way these various types of self-interest interact and the way they pervade our lives, we define the term "Selfonomics." Selfonomics is the study of human behavior,**

individually and in groups, through the lens of all the varieties of self-interest.

CHAPTER 2: TRANSLATING REAL-LIFE SITUATIONS INTO THE LANGUAGE OF SELFONOMICS

Self-interest is in play at every level of individual and collective existence. It motivates me when I am alone, it is present and drives me when I act in a group setting. Viewed in the aggregate, Self-interest reflects the character of small and large groups of people. This extends to towns, states, countries, religions and political parties, as well as community, common interest and social/activity groups.

Self-interest is *always* operating, one way or the other, consciously or not consciously.[22] I see "not conscious" as the product of rote learning, or as a habit formed after many repetitions of the same behavior. In vivo, real life situations can be analyzed in terms of the various kinds of self-interest. Witness the following analysis of my own behavior on a morning of no particular consequence. In parentheses, appear the varieties of self-interest discussed in the last chapter, mainly Direct and Protective Self-Interest (DSI and PSI).

I get up willingly around 7:30 and come out to the kitchen (DSI). There are dishes in the sink. I don't really want to do them, but straightening up has sort of become expected of me (by my wife) if I get out to the kitchen first. So I overcome my wish to ignore the dishes because I wish to avoid my wife's displeasure more (PSI), and selfishly want her

---

[22] I prefer not to use the word "unconscious" because it has a certain associations with psychodynamic theory.

to make me some oatmeal (DSI), without throwing up to me that I don't do my share.

I also avoid starting the day on the wrong foot with her complaining how messy the kitchen is (PSI). (I've been well-trained.) These behaviors, though initiated by self-interest, have become habitual so that I don't have to think about them each day.

I put up coffee first (I love coffee) (DSI) and do dishes and turn on the computer while it's brewing (DSI+PSI). Looking forward to opening email (DSI). Thinking about the stock market, hoping it goes up or at least not down (DSI). Print out some project that should be fun to show to a friend later in the day (DSI). Plan to ask wife what's for dinner because if I don't, that decision will be made at 7:00 p.m. and we won't eat until much later (PSI). I prefer eating earlier and at a predictable time (around 6:30) every night (DSI). I'm a creature of habit and it gives me something to look forward to (DSI).

I hurry to write what I'm writing now because my son will soon invade the kitchen, where I'm typing. I usually enjoy his company (DSI), but when he's here and talking to me, I can't concentrate enough to put these sentences together (PSI). I calculate how much time I need to shower and dress so I can leave the house, do some errands (DSI) and get to the office on time (DSI). I don't like to be late. It makes me uncomfortable (PSI).

We don't think about self-interest all the time, yet it guides our actions. We go to work every day, take a shower every day, and go to sleep around the same time every day. At some point we get into a "habit," and establish behavior that is in our self-interest (or at least we think it is) and we don't question it any more. These habits are similar to incumbent politicians; they are difficult to get out of office. Automatic actions simplify life and also result in an old horse that wants little part of new tricks. Note that the same routine is sprinkled with both DSI and PSI actions. Sometimes they are both clearly involved in the same behavior and sometimes it's hard to tell if more DSI or more PSI is involved in a particular behavior. But everything is ISI, or in my individual self-interest (ISI).

Some group situations can be analyzed from the perspective of the discrete individuals that comprise the group. Consider the following business meeting, where we look for the self-interest motives of attendees, one at a time:

Twelve people are sitting around a large rectangular table at a weekly business unit meeting. Several of the attendees, ones who are on the "fast track," are really into the meeting. They contribute ideas and seem thoroughly engaged in the process. A few others, fearful of losing their jobs, are thinking about how they can "score points." They will have very few novel ideas, and spend their time thinking about what they should be saying and when to say it. They will agree with those around the table that they believe possess power. A few may be totally disinterested in the meeting and are zoning out and thinking about their personal problems, or looking forward to what they'll do with their weekend (despite appearing to pay attention to what is going on).

One may be silently criticizing, perhaps even despising, the director who's running the meeting, believing that he or she has been treated unfairly and overlooked for promotion or a raise. A couple might even be playing "footsie" under the table or trying to make eye contact with someone to whom they are attracted and, perhaps, fantasizing about a liaison. One may be focused on what needs to be done after this meeting, or is bored to tears, or feels that there is no reason to be in attendance, and casts surreptitious glances at her watch every few minutes. And, of course, several of these thought patterns may occur in one given person at various points in the meeting.

This time, self-interest operates in each person and plays off the self-interest of others. Some of the behavior serves a person's DSI, by using the meeting to "get ahead" or increase productivity. Some use it to protect their job by aligning with the powerful people in the room (PSI). Some use it think about other things, including hooking up (DSI and perhaps MSI). They are all acting in their perceived self-interest to move toward something they want, or avoid something they fear (getting fired). It can be conscious, in that some are really trying to solve a business problem, or not conscious, in that the behavior of agreeing with power has become automatic or habitual (which may be seen by others as "sucking up") or one might just mentally drift away from the topic under discussion to something more pleasant.

GROUP SELF-INTEREST OR GSI

Looking at actual group behavior requires some assumptions, namely that (1) people join groups that are consistent with their own individual self-interests, (2) the individual self-interests of the group members will combine to produce and guide the self-interest of the group, (3) the group will then reflect the self-interests of the group members and (4) the group self-interest will then be espoused by individual members of the group.

For example, I join a running club because I enjoy jogging. The frequency, length and difficulty of the group runs will reflect the needs of the members. The group will then be known as anywhere from a powderpuff club to a professional training club. And the participants will talk to others about the kind of running group of which they are a member.

Let's examine some current situations (as of the begining of 2012) involving groups of people and "translate" them into the language of self-interest.

FRACKING AND HOME RULE IN N.Y. STATE

"Fracking" is short for hydraulic fracturing, a method of extracting natural gas from oil shale by pumping a chemically treated liquid deep into the ground, which produces cracks in the rocks and releases gaseous products. The extent of the shale deposits throughout the country holds the promise of decades of cheap clean energy.[23] The catch is that the chemically treated liquid might damage the water supply and eventually harm fauna and flora.

In central western New York State (in an area that includes and surrounds Cooperstown, in the Finger Lakes region), fracking has become a contentious issue on at least two levels. There is a group of people that see this as a way to reduce energy prices, cut carbon emissions (natural gas is relatively clean burning) and reduce our dependence on foreign oil. On the opposite side are environmentalists, who consider the presence of tanker truck traffic and heavy construction vehicles as increasing

---

[23] An example is the Marcellus Shale formation, comprised of huge deposits covering most of Pennsylvania, and large parts of New York and Ohio. See: http://marcelluscoalition.org/

carbon emissions, and fear the effects of the process on our water supply, plants and animals.

The second level is ostensibly purely a money issue. A small number of people, who were fortunate enough to hold land that is attractive to energy companies (the frackers if you will), or were sage enough to purchase land in the hope that fracking would go forward, want to benefit from their good fortune. They stand to make a money in proportion to the amount and location of their land. Everyone else in the region, those that do not own large chunks of acreage, fear that their lifestyle will be quite adversely affected with no hope for anything positive coming out of it.[24]

The fracking/no-fracking issue is not at all unique. The "not in my back yard" philosophy is a common issue that pops up when mental health or alcohol treatment centers are proposed for the suburbs, but are opposed by local community groups trying to protect their children; or when Arizonans and Texans react differently to crimes that are committed by illegal immigrants than do residents of states with a less diverse population; or when residents of states bordering an ocean seek funds to repair beachfront erosion and landlocked states don't want to pay for it with Federal funds.

In each case, it is unclear what the right answer is or, if in fact, there is a right answer. The only thing that seems to be clear is that different groups of people have different self-interests, different GSIs, that drive these disagreements. Resolution of these differences often reverts to the laws of the land, ranging from local ordinances to those set down and/or implied by our Constitution.

---

[24] "New York Takes Up Fracking Issue." NPR Morning Edition, November 3, 2011, with host Steve Inskeep. Reporter: David Chanatry. The show reports on home rule in Dryden, N.Y. which will vote on whether or not to allow fracking. Home rule is the right of a community to dictate what goes on within its borders.

WORLD RICE SUPPLIES[25]

Late in the year 2007, wheat became more expensive in India, so its government made a decision to bar the export of homegrown rice, since it would be needed to feed its own population. This rational decision, with noble intentions, caused less rice to be available on the world market, and rice prices immediately shot up. In reaction, other Asian nations also started hoarding their own rice, making have-not countries pay more to eat. The higher prices led to corruption, with some people and some governments making a killing on buying and selling.

Note that at no time was there less rice in the world, but panic over supply led to hoarding, price gouging and corruption. Globalization of trade and the interdependence of nations didn't help. All of these acts, by each of the nations, groups within nations, and well placed individuals, resulted from looking out for "them and theirs" or protecting them and theirs against harm from another country's policies. In other words, direct or protective group self-interest, DGSI or PGSI.

TAXING THE "1%"

It goes without saying that the those in the highest income brackets have different self-interests than the rest of us. And those in the top 10% bracket have self-interest that differs from those in, say, the 30-40% bracket. It's a zero sum game; that is, if you get a dollar, that's one less dollar available to me and vice versa.

That aside, is it wise to place an additional tax on the top 1% (or top .1% for that matter)? The argument against raising taxes on the rich is that they will stop creating jobs.

------

[25] "How Fear Drove World Rice Markets Insane" From NPR show All Things Considered, November 2, 2011 with host Robert Siegel. Story by Dan Charles.

Or they will move out of a highly taxed location (New York city) to one that takes away less of their money.

Selfonomics predicts that taxing the wealthy a bit more will make no difference in their behavior. First, they will still be making tons of money. Perhaps slightly less. If they are doing so well as to be in the top 1%, it would be against their DSI to make any significant changes in their extant financial behavior since it obviously works quite well for them. As far as changing locale, tax disincentives would have to be an awful lot higher (perhaps 10% or more) for anyone to consider making radical changes in their lifestyle by moving away. Remember, these are the people that don't *need* the money. They live where they *want* to live; if they didn't, they would have moved already.

There is also a question of whether the ultra-rich are ultra-fast at creating jobs. Yes, they will use their "extra" money to invest in something, say equities, that over time will enrich them further and some members of the upper-middle class (stockholders) by pushing stock prices up. More money will also find its way to the financial people who handle these transactions, and eventually will filter down to the lower financial strata, but the velocity of money circulation by this route is slow.

Those that are likely to create jobs more rapidly are small business owners, plumbers and electricians, retailers and restaurateurs, physicians and clinic owners. And, if one wants to get money circulating in the economy in the quickest manner, the people at the bottom of the income ladder will do it the best. They will spend, or recirculate, every last dollar they earn, or receive, on necessities right away, creating jobs almost immediately.

THE "OCCUPY" MOVEMENT

Looking at the myriad of people that joined the Occupy movement, they seem to be cut from a variety of cloths. Many are young and out of work, some are middle aged and out of work, and some are retired. Some are young idealists, some are oldsters reliving their hippie or Vietnam protest days, some are bitter ex-employees or ex-homeowners, some have always been poor and never had assets to lose.

The one thing that almost all *must* have in common is that they are not working. This provides clues as to their self-interests. Occupying, protesting, attending, serves their DSI very well. It gives them a place to go, a social life, free food, a good deal of camaraderie (from what I've read), and is generally a lot more enjoyable than sitting home watching television. It gives them a cause, something to believe in, something to work for that is useful and constructive. They are contributing to society, they feel, by pointing out the flaws in the system.

PSI is also served simultaneously. Whatever resumes needed to be sent out have been sent, job applications have been filled out, and the results have been disappointing. Sitting home, a person feels like a failure, is looked on by parents or partners as a loser. And may be the target of complaints and/or nagging. What does this do to a person's ego over time? Occupying, fighting for a cause is noble, and avoids the ignobility of being the person that no one wants to hire. Being among kindred spirits also provides the comfort of not feeling alone in their malaise. They are supported and appreciated for any chores done around "camp," they are made to feel important by the attention of the media. Their egos are shored up. Pure PSI.

PENN STATE

For those of us who were in a coma in the early part of November of 2011, something terrible happened at Penn State University. It is alleged that an ex-assistant football coach named Jerry Sandusky sodomized young boys over a period of years, ostensibly using a charity he founded as a means to that end. As this s was being written, further details of the case were emerging.[26] But assuming the crimes did occur, certain themes emerge.

Consider all the people surrounding the perpetrator, who either viewed the rape(s) directly or were undeniably aware of them. These include, but are not limited to, the young assistant coach (graduate assistant at the time that witnessed one of the alleged acts),   Joe Paterno, the God of Penn State football (by repute the most important person on campus), the two people above him that he told what happened (the Athletic Director and a Senior Vice President of the University), the President of the University, etc. Each kept quiet, merely passing the information along to someone else in the school's hierarchy. Why? How could any of them conscience the rape of boys without calling the police?

The answer is that *each of them followed their protective self-interest, their PSI.* Every one had similar cost-reward balance sheets floating around in their heads.

1) By telling someone else in authority (the young assistant coach telling Paterno, Paterno telling the Athletic Director, the A.D. telling the president of the University, and perhaps the President telling someone or some ones on the Board of Directors) each could think that they had done what was right, passing the responsibility to someone who had more authority to take appropriate measures.
2) Anyone who was seen as having brought this story to light (calling the police, contacting newspapers) ran the risk of becoming a *pariah* at the school. The perpetrator was a well-respected member of the Penn State community, so the whistleblower might even fear being disbelieved.

------

[26] Timeline of incidents available at: http://articles.cnn.com/2011-11-16/justice/justice_pennsylvania-coach-abuse-timeline_1_grand-jury-report-business-gary-schultz-young-boy?_s=PM:JUSTICE

3) If believed, each knew that this would blow Penn State football, the University and certainly an individual career out of the water.
4) Each must have hoped or thought that the problem would not come out in public, had already been taken care of, or would not be blamed on them.

Similar rationalizations appear in an article by Paul Douthat in the New York Times. Referring to the Catholic Church, "I suspect [that an instinct to shepherd and protect their mission] prompted the higher-ups at Penn State to basically ignore what they described as Jerry Sandusky's "inappropriate conduct," and persuaded Paterno that by punting the allegation to his superiors he had fulfilled his responsibility to the victimized child. He had so many important duties, after all, and so many people counting on him. And Sandusky had done so much good over the years ..."[27]

Does that make each or any of the members of this conspiracy of silence bad people? How about the members of the Catholic Church who knew about sexual abuse by priests but tried to deal with it within the hierarchy rather than call in the authorities? How about the "codes of silence" attributed to law enforcement organizations? Or the people who failed to call police in the apocryphal Kitty Genovese murder case[28] or continued to "shock" subjects in Stanley Milgram's[29] psychology experiments? Are we all subject to this "bystander effect?" Selfonomics tends to look at all these situations in terms of the self-interest of the participants.

---

[27] Douthat, Ross. "The Devil and Joe Paterno." New York Times Op-Ed November 13, 2011.

[28] See: http://www.homicidesquad.com/kitty_genovese.htm

[29] See: http://psychology.about.com/od/historyofpsychology/a/milgram.htm

Freakonomics Radio looked into this very subject.[30] Two famous experiments in social psychology were performed by Stanley Milgram and Philip Zimbardo. Milgram got college students to administer shocks of increasing strength to other people that they could not see but could hear. They obeyed the experimenter's requests to continue despite the plaints of the shock-ees. Zimbardo randomly divided students into jailers and prisoners and locked them away in a college basement for two weeks. The jailers soon started ordering the prisoners around and generally were abusive. The experiment was stopped less than half way through for this reason. Both studies were conducted in the aftermath of World War II and concluded that ordinary people could do horrible things to other humans given the right set of circumstances.

Steve Levitt, Dubner's partner in crime, believes that the results were spurious because the guards were fulfilling the expectations of the experimenters. The participating students would not do this in real life so therefore the results are biased.

Looking at it from the perspective of self-interest yields a different conclusion. Yes, they were trying to please the experimenter by carrying out instructions. But this is the same as trying to curry favor with the "Man" or at least to avoid running into trouble with him. The guards in Zimbardo's experiment saw their self-interest lying with playing their role fully, regardless of the reason. They were "protected" against consequences by the prison administrator (who was Zimbardo) and the fact that they were in an official college study sponsored by the college. They were relieved of responsibility for bad events and rewarded by the professor for cooperation.

The same obtains with people who knowingly gave mortgages to those who couldn't afford them or those who bundled bad investments (credit default swaps) and then bet they'd lose value (financial crisis). It's easier to look out

---

[30] Freakonomics Radio Podcast, rebroadcast on Jan. 16, 2014.

for your self-interest if you are rewarded, protected from responsibility, anonymous or all of the above. (It must be noted that not all experimental subjects cooperated. Some balked.) Analyses of the Kitty Genovese situation and Milgram's experiment follow the same line.

Selfonomics argues that these are *not* bad people. They are merely human. Not many of us would do something different given a similar set of circumstances, despite thinking that we would. Unfortunately or fortunately, self-interest (and/or self-preservation which is extreme PSI) is built into us. Every one of the actors discussed above evaluated the costs and rewards to themselves of their actions and many opted for behavior that is hurtful to others. Their PSI prevailed.

Chapter 3: Assumptions Underlying Selfonomics

Self-Interest is biological, instinctual and genetic

On a common sense basis, as we have evolved as a species, those with better survival instincts lived to reproduce. Those whose survival instincts were less well developed, perished. Let's posit a hominid that walked around 40,000 years ago, and call him Caveman Bob. Bob's life was shorter, simpler, and a lot more focused than ours is today. He spent almost all of his time hunting and gathering food, providing shelter, tending to his family, defending his brood from predators, human and otherwise, and not much else. Self-interest was clear and uncomplicated; survival.

Survival involves both direct and protective self-interest. The strongest, fastest and wiliest humans (and perhaps the most physically appealing) caught and killed more game, ate better, were the leaders of their tribes and repoduced more easily. That's DSI. But what about PSI?

The WNYC radio show, "Radio Lab," hosted by Jad Abumrad, aired an episode entitled "One Eye Open."[31] The show describe reptiles, birds and aquatic mammals that sleep one half of a brain at a time by keeping one of their eyes open. This allows for rest and protection at the same time. At some point the sides switch so that the entire brain gets the necessary rest. This is a way of reducing "predation risk," simply put, the odds of getting eaten by a

---

[31] http://www.radiolab.org/story/91529-one-eye-open/

predator.[32][33]   The better an organism protects itself from becoming food for another organism, the better its odds of survival and procreation. In fact, DSI and PSI have to be in balance for each species for it to survive and, on the other extreme, not take over the world.

The survival motive, which was obviously in Bob's self-interest, was honed since man walked upright and, if you think about it, since the existence of the first living organism. Primitive organisms that had more of a "self-interest drive" built into their DNA, meaning they were better suited to compete for resources, survived to reproduce; the meek, or those that were the poorer hunters or less able defenders, perished. If we believe in evolution, by definition, our DNA has evolved to support self-interest.[34]   Has it changed over the last 40,000 years since the time of Caveman Bob? Perhaps the ratio of brain to brawn has increased a little, but otherwise not so much.

Have the Anno Domini years been any different? Almost all humans that have ever lived worked hard and long to satisfy the most basic of needs of food, clothing and

---

[32] http://en.wikipedia.org/wiki/Predation

[33] **Two examples.** Dolphins are aquatic mammals that need to breathe air. How do they breathe and sleep at the same time? Turns out that half of their brain sleeps at a time. One half lets the dolphin rest, the other keeps it swimming to the surface to get air. It's called "unispheric

sleep." Imagine four ducks lined up on a log. The two in the middle have both eyes closed, the two on the outside have one eye open, the eye that faces the outside to guard against predators. They periodically change places.

[34] This is analogous to the existence of any business. Instead of self-interest honed by DNA, businesses exist to make money. If they are good at making money, they continue to exist. If they fail at this task, they fold, or "die off." This is one reason that expecting businesses to create jobs is a futile unless those jobs help them make more money. If hiring people will not increase profits (or lessen losses) adding staff will not occur.

shelter. Throughout the last two millennia, most were illiterate, poor and overworked. Only the cream of society had access to the finer things in life and the time to appreciate them. And these elite acted in their own self-interest as well, if only to maintain their privileged positions.

Although today we can look well beyond food and shelter, the self-interest motive doesn't appear to have changed much in modern times. The average person of the twenty-first century will still be faced with physical needs as well as safety needs and desires to be social and respected within their communities. All of these speak of, and are driven by, self-interest.

A Personal Experience in Getting Close to Instinctual Self-Interest

Major spinal surgery requires spine.   Fusion at L4-L5, laminectomies from L-1 to S-1. Woke up in a fog of morphine. I define pain levels from 1 to 10. One or two, I can sleep with.   Three through six are real pain. Five or six, no sleep, no how; three or four, maybe, depending on how tired I am. I don't use seven through ten. They are reserved for sharp acute jabs, spasms or jolts that last a second or so, and that leave me scared. I haven't experienced too many of them, but just enough to keep me obeying doctor's orders not to bend, lift or twist.

The first few days in the hospital were helped by a morphine pump, which gave relief within a minute. The last two days in the hospital and the first few days at home were difficult. My pain level varied from three to six at all times. Pain would decrease for an hour or so after a pair of Percasets that could be taken every three to four hours, allowing me to drift into a welcome stupor.

My world, very simply, involved calculations about how to reduce pain. Lie on one side for an hour, and the pain level would slowly creep up from a three to a five, the point at which it became "worth it" to go through the greater pain of turning to get into another position. There, the pain was a six initially, until it "calmed down" and sank to a three for an hour or so. Lying on my side, moving my top leg forward or back of my bottom leg by a single inch might make a difference.

The back discomfort was complicated by a different kind of pain; the urge to urinate or defecate, and not knowing which. I would abide it, until the abdominal pain got worse than the back pain, and then would get up and use a walker to trudge to the raised potty in the bathroom. Getting up and down from toilet or bed was initially agonizing (higher than six), urinating was painful and defecation didn't occur, despite urges. I would get cold and somehow this was painful too, but reaching down to pull up the blanket was more painful so the cold was endured. Each waking hour of each day was spent this way; attempting to go from a higher pain level to a lower pain level. Pure protective self-interest.

In this state, nothing else but pain reduction bore any importance. My wife, an unbelievably good caretaker, was seen as a route to reduce pain. If she disappointed me, by fumbling with my back brace for too long, thus increasing the duration of pain, I barked at her impatiently. Apologized, and felt guilty, but at the time had trouble restraining my frustration at not being able to reduce pain quickly enough.

First night home, four days after the operation, I asked for three of my favorite things; a small salad, a steak and a glass of wine. Couldn't ingest any of the three. The beef turned my stomach. I have no idea why. The only thing that appealed to me for a few days were tangerine sections and plain water. My biology, the organism attached to my brain, seemed to be speaking to me, saying "protect yourself," "just eat what you can," "don't push it." None of the usual favorite activities were of interest; crossword puzzles, computer projects, current events, sports on television. I wanted to talk to no one, despite knowing that friends were asking about how I was feeling. Everything was about self-protection and minimizing or avoiding pain.

Looking back, I see this as the human condition, wearing no makeup. No socially acceptable responses, no rationalizations for why I am taking care of number one, no pretense of caring about others. Biological and instinctual self-interest, displayed by an organism intent on survival. That would be me.

SELF-INTEREST AND PARENTAL LOVE

One potential speed bump for a theory of all-pervasive self-interest is how do we account for parent-child love, where most parents put their children before themselves? There is nothing quite as rewarding as a toddler running up to a parent with his or her arms in the air, saying "Up!" Rewarding for the parent as well as the child, and serving the self-interest of both. I also know from experience that as a parent, I have done things for my children expecting nothing back in return. I do recognize that there are plenty of times I've done things to make myself feel good as a parent (that I'm doing my job as a parent) or to get love back in return from the child (which makes *me* feel good) or to just get them to keep quiet. In general when they are happy, we are happy, and our direct self-interest is served. When they are hurt or unhappy, we are also.[35]

The theory of self-interest, all the time, explains parent-child love by assuming that we see our children as

---

[35] "Given a choice between self-interest and the greater good, voters will usually watch out for themselves — unless that greater good is their own family." From: Egan, Timothy. "The Need for Greed." New York Times Op-Ed, May 16, 2011. Egan's column deals with the unpopularity of Paul Ryan's plan to replace Medicare with a voucher system.

extensions or parts of ourselves, looking out for them *as if they were us*. This makes sense on an evolutionary basis, since parents who protected/loved their children more continued to advance their blood lines, while those nuclear families with weaker parental instincts died out.[36]

It may just be that Darwinian instinct to love without much in return that keeps us from running away from our parental duties, or from throwing the little tikes out the car window. Pets may fall in the same category, being child-surrogates. Personally, I am very taken with my dog, and the attention she gives me when I come home serves my self-interest. My self-interest is also served if I can avoid three things: poop, pee and barking. I clean up the messes because they stink or will get dragged around the floor if I don't. I walk the pup to avoid mop duty. And I feed her to avoid being barked to distraction. All of these serve my self-interest.

In effect, parents look out for their children as they do for themselves, until the children are ready to take over that job. To that end, parents teach their children how to look out for themselves, how to defend themselves, how not to let others take advantage of them. They teach the skills needed to survive in the society in which they will grow up. They also instill rules that are necessary to curb their own feral, unbridled self-interest. Thus we learn to brush our teeth, eat vegetables, get enough sleep and attend school.

We are not born knowing *not* to steal. We learn parameters to govern our self-interest; that is, it is okay to want something, but we must say "please" and "thank you" to get it. These magic words help disguise self-interest and hide it from both the asker and the one asked. Rules, primarily taught by parents, curb, direct and guide our instinctive self-interest. In fact, learning these rules and

---

[36] Dawkins, R. (2006). *The Selfish Gene (30th Anniversary Edition)*. New York City: Oxford University Press.

guidelines actually improves the chance, that over the long run, we'll get what we want.

IT IS ASSUMED THAT PEOPLE ARE LOGICAL CREATURES

It is assumed that people are logical and make rational decisions. Not necessarily accurate ones, but logical. Look at the following two syllogisms:

>All men are mortal,
>Socrates is a man,
>Therefore, Socrates is mortal.

>All men are elephants,
>Socrates is a man,
>Therefore, Socrates is an elephant.

Both result in logical conclusions. In the first case, the conclusion is logical and true. In the second, the conclusion is logical but false. The point is that we can all be logical, but if we start from false premises, we will end up with false conclusions. More often, we start with premises that are just matters of opinion (choice of car, favorite food, Democrat/Republican).

As an example, if one believes that life begins at the moment of conception, then abortion is killing. If another believes that life begins at the moment of birth, abortion is not killing. Given a belief one way or the other, conclusions are logically reached, again one way or the other.

Humans walk around with networks of premises in their heads and put them together in a logical way to choose behaviors. Behaviors are conclusions to the syllogisms, and are what can be observed. Self-interest, in its variants within a person, needs to be surmised from that observed behavior. In effect, we have to *induce* the premises from the conclusions that we see.

Since each of us thinks logically, but is operating on a different subset of premises about a particular subject, we will reach differing conclusions. Unfortunately, it is quite common for one person to see another person's conclusions, which are opinions, as wrong, crazy, stupid, irrational, malicious, or some combination thereof. Of course, we're the only ones who are right, ethical, well-intentioned and rational.

INDUCING SELF-INTEREST

By making the assumption that all people are logical we can understand and predict their behavior better if we can unearth their premises, including the flavors of self-interest on which they act (DSI/PSI/MSI).

Reversing the direction of the logical process, that is, instead of deducing conclusions from premises, we try to get at the premises by observing the conclusions, can be less certain. Often, we don't have access to a person's premises, but do know their conclusions, in the form of behavior that we observe. Our job is to figure out what leads a person to behave in a given way. When we know the conclusion, we cannot, with certainty, divine the premises. We're going to have to make educated guesses. Heads up! Incoming shards of high school algebra comin' at you.... (If you hated math in high school, take a black magic marker, color over the next section, and pretend it isn't there.)

In algebra, letters stand for unknown numbers. Think X, Y and Z. You can "solve" an equation, meaning figure out what X stands for, if you have the same number of unknowns as equations. Thus, if $X + 4 = 5$, we know that $X = 1$. In fact X MUST equal one. With two unknowns and two equations, such as $X + Y = 5$ and $X - Y = 1$, we can figure out that X must equal 3 and Y must equal 2.

But what if we have more unknowns that we do equations? For example, we have the equation $X + Y = 3$. One equation, two unknowns. Can we figure out the value of X? Or Y? No. The only thing we can do is say something like..."If X=0, then Y=3. If X=1, then Y=2. If X=2, then Y=1, etc" (this can be extended to any value of X, from negative infinity to positive infinity). We know something about the relationship between X and Y, but we don't know anything for sure. If we can get information from another source, e.g., a little birdie tells us that X is an odd positive number that is less than four, we can narrow X down (to X= 1 or X=3). We can now go back to reality...

Starting with a conclusion and trying to figure out what the premises must have been is a lot like having more unknowns than equations. We can narrow down the premises through what we see, and then look for information that will help us home in on specifics. Since I'm a psychologist by trade, let me present a "case study." For the sake of discussion, take the totally hypothetical case of a young lady named Sally. Names have been changed to protect the hypothetical.

Sally wants to end a year long relationship with her boyfriend, whose name is Dan. What can we deduce? First, people don't make these kinds of decisions precipitously. At least most of us don't. So we can guess that Sally has been thinking about it for a while. Second, the relationship must have worked for her for a period of time, else why would she have stayed for a year. Because she stayed for a year, she must have been weighing the pluses and minuses of the relationship.

At the six-month mark, the scale may have tilted in the direction of staying with Dan, but by the year mark, she's ready to pull the plug. Assuming they are both in their twenties, what might be some of the factors that enter into her decision. In other words, what were the premises rattling around in Sally's brain to induce the conclusion of "Gotta go?"

Some educated guesses would be Dan doesn't earn enough money, doesn't communicate well enough, drinks too much, doesn't get along with her family, isn't attractive enough to her, is disrespectful or downright abusive, is too possessive, has cheated, watches too many ball games, puts his friends before her, etc. When you think about it, the choices aren't infinite. Dan's strengths are what kept her in the relationship for so long. For example, he may earn lots of money, or be very affectionate, or attentive, or gets along great with her Dad and family, or is kind and responsible. Or, he may be the only guy who has shown any interest in dating Sally. Again, not an infinite array of choices. If you had access to Sally for an hour, my guess is a few strategic questions would let you get a pretty good picture of her reasons, or premises.

Although these educated guesses don't give us a complete picture of Sally's decision, it will be pretty close. And pretty close is about as close as anyone can get to anyone else's thoughts. For a person in therapy, each session gives the therapist a chance to fill out the picture with more information. The filled-out picture allows the client and therapist to see if there are beliefs and repetitive patterns in a person's behavior which may not work very well for them. For example, if Dan was dumped because he drank too much and he is the third guy Sally dumped for the same reason, one might suppose that Sally exercises poor judgment in picking men (or, perhaps, that she drives them all to drink).

The significance of the previous "case study" is that it shows a path by which premises can be induced from conclusions. This is the process by which we can attempt to get at the different kinds and directions of self-interest that people hold.

The relatively new field of behavioral economics offers examples of the importance of inducing self-interest motives from observed behavior. Dan Ariely named his best-seller, "Predictably Irrational," because his experiments found that subjects often reacted in ways that didn't make sense, or were counterintuitive. My belief, and the dictates of Selfonomics, is the opposite. I would've chosen the title, "Unpredictably Rational," since I believe that his subjects made logical decisions based on premises unknown to the experimenter. Once those premises were discovered, the observed behavior made sense.

For example Ariely, toward the end of his book, describes a series of experiments to see whether or not people will cheat if there is no chance that they will be caught. It turns out that they did cheat, but only a little. Apparently, cheaters still have to live with themselves and/ or didn't want it to be obvious to others that they cut corners and/or were able to rationalize away their behavior. When the experimenters asked subjects to recall as many of the Ten Commandments as they could, or were advised that the experiment fell under the school honor code (which didn't exist), the cheating virtually disappeared.

Ariely maintains that this behavior is irrational. It is, but only if you adhere to a strict economic model that demands that rational man must always attempt to maximize *monetary* gain. (To be fair, monetary gain is easily measured whereas other measures of self-interest are much, much harder to operationalize and measure.) In the words used here, it means looking at only Direct Self-Interest, without regard to Protective or Misguided Self-Interest. Since subjects let other influences enter into their decisions to cheat or not to cheat, such as guilt, seeking approval and rationalization, behaviors are emitted that Ariely terms irrational. With Selfonomics, all premises, including maximizing monetary gain, but also including those dictated by conscience or guilt, come into play to reach conclusions that are eminently rational. Ariely, in effect, was glossing over premises that even many of his subjects may not have even known they held.

Both "Predictably Irrational" and the "Freakonomics" series point out that if we are to understand humans we need to seek out the premises on which they act and not just the ones they can or are willing to verbalize. As will be discussed a bit later, self-interest is not something people are necessarily aware of or, if they are aware of it, are not willing or able to discuss. Further, it is likely that the amount of guilt felt by the array of subjects in Ariely's experiment was distributed normally, so that some subjects would be quite influenced by incipient guilt and others not at all. HIgh-guilt and low guilt subjects are averaged by the results. And by mentioning the honor code you are, in effect, adding a layer of guilt onto each subject's existing level of guilt.

Finally, there are three main objections to a theory that proposes that all human action is geared to derive pleasure or avoid pain.[37] They are, the apparent existence of altruism, exceptions to the rule and tautology. Altruism is treated separately in Chapter 11.

---

[37] This has also been dubbed psychological egoism or psychological hedonism.

Exceptions are almost always ultra-rare events and can be explained by other means. "What interest can a fond mother have in view, who loses her health by assiduous attendance on her sick child, and afterwards languishes and dies of grief, when freed (by the child's passing)...?[38] To explain this, we must invoke the notion that the child is part of the mother and she grieves for that child as she would for her own death. This is supported by the Darwinian legacy whereby more concerned parents had larger and more survivable broods.

Another posited rare event is that of a soldier who jumps on a grenade, thus sacrificing his life, in order to save others. First, this is an extremely low-occurrence event. Second, given one hundred of these "opportunities," it would be surprising if even one of them resulted in such sacrifice. Not many people are wired that way. Further, it would be likely that the ones who do sacrifice have preemptively replayed this instant over in their minds and decided that, given the chance, they would give up their lives. In other words, they were pre-programmed, either by their drill sergeants, an heroic ancestor or the promise of heaven. It is even possible that it was done out of protective self-interest, that is to end the horror of battlefield events in much the same way as people jump from burning buildings so as not to be enveloped by flames. Another possibility is that since the hero did not give herself a chance to think through the consequences, so that if more time was available, a different action, such as calling for help or doing nothing may have resulted

That Selfonomics is circular reasoning is not being denied. That doesn't make it wrong. If I ask, "Why do things drop? and receive the answer, "Because of gravity," and then ask, "How do we know about gravity?" and hear, "Because things drop" this is circular reasoning as well.

---

38 Hume, D. (1751). *An Enquiry Concerning the Principles of Morals.* Public domain.

But gravity still exists and we still explain it using the concept of gravity.

CHAPTER 4: WHY WE DON'T TALK ABOUT SELF-INTEREST?

What's the big deal, even if everyone *is* actually looking out for him or herself, all the time? Well, *one big problem is that we just don't, can't or won't see it in ourselves, though we can see it in others quite clearly.* Thanks to my trusty computerized thesaurus, here are some synonyms of the word "selfish":

> egocentric, egomaniacal, egotistic, self-absorbed, self-centered, self-interested, self-serving, conceited, narcissistic, stuck-up

We are all taught that selfish is not a good thing to be. We certainly don't like being *called* selfish. We are all certain that we are *not* selfish. The other guy maybe, but not us. And we're all above average drivers, too.[39] But maybe we're looking up the wrong thing.

Let's try self-interest. It's defined as (1) concern for your own interests and welfare; (2) taking advantage of opportunities without regard for the consequences of others. Okay, not real promising either. Let's look at its synonyms[40]:

> acquisitiveness, autism, careerism, ego, ego trip, egocentricity, egocentrism, egoism, egotisticalness, egotism, egotisticalness, graspingness, greed, individualism, interest, narcissism, personal

---

[39] Attributed to Dave Barry or Garrison Keillor. Take your pick.

[40] From: The Free Online Dictionary and Thesaurus.

aims, personal ambition, personal desires, personalism, possessiveness, privatism, remoteness, self-absorption, self-admiration, self-advancement, self-centeredness, self-centerment, self-consideration, self-containment, self-devotion, self-esteem, self-indulgence,self-interestedness, self-jealousy, self-occupation, self-pleasing, self-seeking, self-serving, self-solicitude, self-sufficiency,

In this list, there are a few that don't sound like we'd cringe if someone referred to us as possessing the trait, such as "individualism" and "self-esteem," but the rest are in the same category as synonyms for "selfish." On balance, we still have to strenuously deny this scurrilous accusation, i.e. "We are not self-interested!"

Since almost all words that describe self-interest are quite negative, we do not have much of a vocabulary to deal with the subject. That is why it was helpful to break down self-interest into components such as DSI, PSI and MSI. And why it is helpful to see self-interest as natural and universal rather than negative and a sign of bad character. As a matter of fact, note that all the terms refer to *Direct* Self-Interest and none to *Protective* Self-Interest.

The universality of self-interest can be counterintuitive. Let's start from the assumption of universal self-interest and see where it takes us. Suppose you call me up to play golf with you on Saturday. Why? Because I'm a really nice guy? Because you're a really nice guy and want to get me out of the house and show me a good time? I don't think so. My bet is on....because *you* want to play golf. I don't think that's a big assumptive leap. Why call *me*? Do you go through the rolodex in your mind just to see who needs a break the most? Tom, Dick, or Tony? No. You call the guy whose company *you* will enjoy the most, the guy with whom *you* can have the most fun, the guy that you know will be free this Sunday, or the guy whose golf game matches your own for mediocrity. You're not doing *me* any favors, you're doing something that *you* want to do. Similarly, if I'm dumb enough to agree to play golf with you, it's because *I* want to play golf. And, because I have no better offers, I'll say yes to you. We're *both* acting in our own self-interest!

More broadly, why would I want *you* for a friend? To make *you* happy? No. To make *me* happy. I move into a new neighborhood (by the way, I'm doing this soliloquy as if I were single, which I'm not, just to keep things simple). None of the men know each other. How do the friendships form? Primarily, assuming we all live close to one another, I will choose for friends those guys that I get along with the best. Meaning the ones I like the best. Other factors might be befriending those that share my interests (golf, lawn care, poker, adolescent humor, doo-wop music), or live immediately next door so that they can watch my house and pick up my mail/newspapers if I go on vacation (being "altruistic," I'm willing to reciprocate), or have kids the same age as mine so we can toss a ball around together, or those who have neat power tools that they are willing to lend out to a great neighbor. Notice that I may think that me and Ralph have a great rapport goin' (i.e. he meets my needs), but Ralph may think I'm a jerk and avoid me like the plague (and meet his own needs). And nowhere in these examples, do any of the actors recognize that they are behaving in their own self-interest. We all think that we act reasonably and that we always take the "high road."

Even love fits the model. Romeo digs Juliet, really digs her. He flat out pines for her, aches for her. He'll drive (in his chariot, of course) miles out of his way to meet her for a cup of coffee. He'll spend money he doesn't have to take her out, to buy her flowers, to attract and impress her. Why? I would argue that, just as Romeo gets hungry, and the only thing that will reduce that discomfort is to eat, the only way to sate his besotted soul is to see his love. *He*, Romeo, feels better. We can only hope, for his sake, that Juliet is smitten also. Juliet meets *his* internalized vision of the perfect hourglass-shaped woman; she meets *his* need to find the right woman to settle down with and raise his children with; she is perfect in his eyes. Is this love selfless or an abject display of direct self-interest?

Similarly Juliet, taught from childhood that one must not only have a career, but must find a mate, is looking for that guy of her dreams. She has an image of the courtship, the engagement ring, the wedding, the Roman ruin with the white picket fence and offspring instilled in her. All she needs is a guy to fill the role of life partner. And, at a party, when she meets Romeo and his immature friends Lefty and Chuck, her heart flutters at the sight of Romeo. A diamond in the rough. A husband in the making. What ensues is not what's good for Romeo (although again, we hope it's reciprocal), but what's good for *her*.[41]

Summing up so far, it seems that all people act in their self-interest all of the time, even though none of us recognizes it as such, with the caveat that we include our children under the umbrella of "self." We choose golf partners, friends, people to date, and even spouses on the basis of what's good for us. This invokes a much wider definition of the word selfish than is generally held. *Being selfish is apparently not bad. It is eminently human, as is the tendency to not see it.*

Indirect proof of the invisibility of self-interest is offered, in a backwards way, by the Sapir-Whorf Hypothesis, or the principle of linguistic relativity. The standard example is that Eskimos have many words for snow in their language, while the rest of us Americans have but one. Implied is that Eskimos think more often and with more complexity about snow than we do.

There are few words, most of which are listed at the beginning of this chapter to describe the meaning of self-interest. And most words on that list all have a negative

---

[41] The same point is made in an article by Tara Parker-Pope: "The Happy Marriage is the 'Me' Marriage." New York Times, December 31, 2010.

connotation, which carries the implication that we don't want those words applied to ourselves. Self-interest, in *the context used here,* is *not* negative; merely human. The absence of many good descriptors of this non-negative concept, which I believe, underlies all human behavior, implies that we don't think about self-interest often or in depth.

Is all snow the same to us? Perhaps, but all self-interest is certainly not. The self-interest involved in making money to support our family, in choosing friends, in protecting ourselves and loved ones from burglars by putting locks on the doors, in avoiding social situations that are uncomfortable for us, are surely all different. Yet we just don't have shades of meaning for a phrase that permeates and pervades our society and our lives. So on rare occasions that we do speak about self-interest, the term has a negative connotation and is applied to others, not to ourselves.

What we end up doing is speaking euphemistically about self-interest. These are some of the phrases that are commonly used:

What's in it for him?

What's his angle?

What's the hidden agenda?

What's his game?

He always needs to be in control. He's a manipulator. (i.e. he wants things done *his* way, in *his* self-interest)

He's very bossy.

He has an ulterior motive.

Believe what he does, not what he says.

He has to walk the walk, not just talk the talk.

All of the above have distinctly negative connotations. All of the above are said of others, but never of ourselves. All don't recognize that looking out for oneself is a normal and natural way to behave. Though all of our behavior is driven by self-interest, it is not polite or socially acceptable to show it. As a result, much of our behavior revolves around developing ways to *not* show it, such as rationalization, denial (and other classic "defense mechanisms"), as well as the rules of etiquette and fair play. In fact, the teachings of all major religions involve rules for limiting, suppressing or denying our self-interest. The Emperor is not wearing any clothes, but it is always impolite to say so.

So what, you ask?

What's the big deal if we don't recognize our own self-interest? Or are not used to talking about self-interest? Does it really matter?

Well, let's look first at other subjects that duck under our radar. In 2009, Charles Blow wrote an Op-Ed in response to Attorney General Eric Holder's assertion that we were "a nation of cowards" because we don't have open and honest discussions about race.[42] Blow then reports on polls and studies on the subject of race:

---

[42] Blow, Charles. "A Nation of Cowards?" New York Times Op-Ed, February 20, 2009.

70

"...twice as many blacks as whites thought racism was a big problem in this country, while twice as many whites as blacks thought that blacks had achieved racial equality."

"...72 percent of whites thought that blacks overestimated the amount of discrimination against them, while 82 percent of blacks thought that whites underestimated the amount of discrimination against blacks."

"...found that many white doctors also had an implicit pro-white/anti-black bias, while black doctors showed almost no bias for one race or the other. The paper suggested that these biases may contribute to the unequal treatment of blacks, and that doctors may not even be conscious of it."

There are two points of interest from the perspective of our thesis. First is that the racial biases, for the most part, are unrecognized. Why this happens is a subject for another tome and time, but a superficial guess involves "garbage in, garbage out" thinking. And whatever concepts we walk around with *are* us. We don't often question our beliefs.

Second, talking about race is extremely awkward and uncomfortable, especially for whites. "...white people don't want to be labeled as prejudiced, so they work hard around blacks not to appear so. A study conducted by researchers at Tufts University and Harvard Business School and published in the Journal of Personality and Social Psychology found that many whites — including those as young as 10 years old — are so worried about appearing prejudiced that they act colorblind around blacks, avoiding 'talking about race, or even acknowledging racial difference,' even when race is germane. Interestingly, blacks thought that whites who did this were more prejudiced than those who didn't."[43] A similar stance was

---

[43] ibid

admitted by the supervisors of Major Nidal Malik Hasan, the psychiatrist held in the mass murder at Fort Hood, Texas on November 5, 2009. They reported bending over backwards to be supportive because of his faith.

Further, there's been a tacit agreement between Republicans and Democrats. "The two parties, which openly clashed over race from the late 1970s through the mid-1990s, have for the last decade pretty much agreed not to talk about race - a silence that impedes progress toward racial equality."[44] This is especially true in the wake of rising unemployment and home foreclosures which disproportionally affect the pocketbooks of Hispanics and African Americans.

Aside from race, there are other strongly-held beliefs that are not recognized by the person holding them. Low self-esteem, religious prejudice, chauvinism towards women (or men), depression and even less serious ones such as preference of blondes over brunettes, or tall thin people over short heavy ones, often slips under our own radar.

We are also even prejudiced against the ugly. "...being attractive also helps you earn more money, find a higher-earning spouse (and one who looks better, too!) and get better deals on mortgages. Each of these facts has been demonstrated over the past 20 years by many economists and other researchers. The effects are not small: one study showed that an American worker who was among the bottom one-seventh in looks, as assessed by randomly chosen observers, earned 10 to 15 percent less per year than a similar worker whose looks were assessed in the top one-third — a lifetime difference, in a typical case, of about $230,000."[45]

---

[44] King, Desmond S. & Smith, Rogers M. "On Race, the Silence Is Bipartisan." New York Times Op-Ed, September 2, 2011.

[45] Hamermesh, Daniel S. "Ugly? You May Have A Case." New York Times, August 27, 2011.

Even psychotherapists are prone to this bias. "YAVIS" patients (an acronym for young, attractive, verbal, intelligent, successful) tend to receive better treatment from their therapists than do "HOUNDS" (homely, old, unsuccessful, nonverbal, dumb).[46] Unrecognized, undiscussed, un-dealt-with prejudice.

Self-interest is similar. As with racial prejudice and other biases, we do not often recognize our own motivations which, as has been stated before and will be again, are *always* to look out for ourselves. Though we act on self-interest, we don't realize that we do. And while others in multi-person situations (marriage, family, work environment) act on *their* own SI, we often don't see that either. Sometimes, we will think of another as being selfish, or bossy, or manipulative, and see that as a bad thing, not realizing that we *all* do it in different ways and differing degrees and that it would not be normal *not* to do so.

There are life events that are treated with the same unease as is the topic of race. Women who have been molested or worse, or have chosen to have an abortion, are often not eager or comfortable talking about it. Some men or women who have been in prison, or have dropped out of school, have homosexual leanings or have a history of drug usage will often keep that information to themselves. The reasons for reticence vary from embarrassment, to fear of not getting a job, to fear of rejection, or some combination thereof. In effect, *not* talking about these topics serves our self-interest! And often being tight-lipped is *not* misguided self-interest.

Likewise selfishness or self-interest, because of the awkwardness of the topic, rarely enters into public discussion, with the possible exception of when someone is being seen as greedy. It is okay to discuss greed, because

---

[46] Kaswell, Alice Shirrell; Lucille Zimmerman and G. Neil Martin (2001). "It's Good to Be a YAVIS". *Improbable Research*. http://improbable.com/airchives/paperair/volume7/v7i2/yavis-7-2.html

it's the other guy that's greedy, not us. We just try and accumulate as much money as we can to support our family. If we can get extra money, it's just saving for a rainy day, or because we deserve it for all our hard work, or it's for our kids, not us. If the other guy gets extra money, he's just being greedy. Rationalization running amok.

What makes self-interest so hard to discuss even as applied to others? For one, it's not politically correct or socially acceptable to accuse others of looking out for themselves, except in the case of what seems to be outrageous monetary greed (think of CEOs of failing corporations getting big bonuses). Accusing someone of exhibiting self-interest is tantamount to calling them mean, or a jerk, or a crook. Using that language in social conversation is seen as a hostile act. And may lead the speaker to be seen as the offender. So we have to have a very good reason to go in that direction. It usually therefore serves our self-interest to keep our mouths shut.

PART II: SELFONOMICS IN EVERYDAY LIFE

If self-interest operates all the time in all of us, we should be able to point to it in all aspects of our daily lives. The first discussion looks at the role self-interest plays at the various ages and stages of our lives. Then, looking at an average family, we see that various types of self-interest guides all of the family's expenditures. The behavior of individuals, as seen by a psychologist (that's me) in his office, gives us a clue as to how self-interest guides both healthy and unhealthy choices. Finally decision making and disagreements are interpreted through the lens of self-interest.

CHAPTER 5: SELF-INTEREST THROUGH THE LIFE CYCLE

THE EARLY YEARS

The process of maturation fits nicely into the notion that self-interest underlies all human behavior. The early years of our lives are characterized by the interplay of feral needs and the attempts of our parents to teach us to control them. As infants, we are mostly balls of Direct Self-Interest, or DSI, much of which involves either a bottle or being held. Sleeping and crying can be thought of as primitive Protective Self-Interest, or PSI. As we age and understand more, we are taught more rules (PSI). Starting with "No!" and moving on to "Don't touch that," "Don't cross the street," "It's time to go to bed," are all rules or routines that parents teach and enforce.

We are basically hedonistic as children, doing what feels good, eating what tastes good or being attracted to toys that look good. Unless, that is, we are limited to self-activated consequences (we run too fast, fall down and hurt ourselves), our parents tell us not to do something, or prevent us from doing something. We're told that it's too late to go out and play, or to not take a cookie before dinner, or that we will be punished for telling a lie. These rules are instilled early in us, at a time when parents can control us through positive (love, hugs, praise) and negative (censure, punishment, withholding rewards) reinforcers.

If left to our own devices, we will follow our direct self-interest (DSI) alone. We will watch TV, play video games, stay up as late as we can, or until we fall asleep, unless our parents establish and enforce a bedtime. Some parents will let young children have more of a say over their DSI than others, for example by letting them watch as much TV as they want. Since the content found on TV and video games is very exciting, these kids may have a difficult time appreciating more mundane pastimes, such as reading or playing board games. If children are given too wide a berth in choosing their own DSI (fun behaviors), it may be more difficult to control or reign in their choices as the get older. In fact, the internet and the various game systems that children are exposed to, provide far more excitement and variety (including violence and pornography) than older input channels. How this will affect the next generation is certainly uncertain.

We learn the rules that guide, restrain and channel our self-interest concurrent with learning to use the potty, memorizing our numbers and letters, learning to dress ourselves and get better at sports. As we live longer with these rules, we incorporate them into our own set of beliefs that become more and more impervious to change as we age. If we are made to take turns with our younger brother, taking turns becomes a more and more engrained part of our belief system. Later in life, when driving in traffic, we are more likely to be comfortable with alternating traffic when two lanes feed into one. We see people who don't take turns as being rude.

When young, what we do and what we are *not* allowed to do is all we know. As we learn to express and channel our DSI in certain ways, they become part of the network of beliefs that *is* us. If our Dad watches baseball with us, takes us to an occasional game and has a catch with us a few times a week, we are likely to grow up liking baseball, fulfilling our DSI through it. We may continue as a player if we meet with some success, and continue our interest in fandom as we age.

If we are not allowed to play video games because our parents say it's not good for us, we will accept it when young and eventually be more likely to espouse that same view. As we get older, we will not have much in common with kids that do play those games, and choose other friends that like activities that we participate in. The beliefs of "baseball is good," and "video games are not" will become part of us. The longer we hold these beliefs, the more impervious they are to change. We only grow up in one house (usually) and are taught one set of rules that we don't often question. Wouldn't do much good if we did. For young children, parents are all-powerful, and it takes a lot to get us to think that the way we were raised was flawed (at least until we become teenagers or adults).

Only knowing or having one set of rules to grow up with may be a distinct advantage in learning to respect authority. In a family where there is one set of rules before the parents divorce, two sets of rules (for each household) after the divorce, and perhaps a different two sets upon the re-coupling of the parents, it's likely that children will choose "the path of least resistance," following their DSI to get the best deal for themselves. Once a ten year old is allowed to stay up late or play video games under the aegis of one parent's rule set, it's difficult to get them to go to bed earlier or give up the games. As the old song goes, "How 'Ya Gonna Keep 'Em Down on the Farm? (After They've Seen Paree).[47]

The psychologically most important category (or cluster) of beliefs we hold about ourselves concerns our self-image, which develops over the years. Whether or not we think we are a "good boy," or "good girl," foretells how we will express our DSI as we get older. If we feel that we can't be rewarded for being the smartest, because of our genius big sister, or the best athlete, like our jock big brother, we may be tempted to get attention, and/or have fun, by being the brattiest. Oddly, getting negative attention from parents is better than getting none at all. The class clown in third grade is actually having fun, which is DSI, until she finds out later on that the behavior is misguided (MSI) when negative consequences occur. If

---

[47] Lyrics by Joe Young and Sam M. Lewis, melody by Walter Donaldson, published in 1918.

they don't occur, or if those negative consequences are not motivating enough to outweigh the attention of classmates, the behavior may continue.

Gradually, school takes over to teach us more rules. While our unfettered self-interest might lead us to want to play with all the toys and run around the classroom, we conform to avoid censure from teachers and parents, and humiliation from the barbs of other students. By conforming to the rules, we learn to pay attention in class, or at least look like we're paying attention in class. Whether we're actually paying attention or daydreaming might depend (by degrees) on whether we like the subject and/or teacher, understand what's going on, seek approval for good behavior or try to avoid punishment for bad behavior.

School further limits and channels our DSI while increasing our PSI. Initially, we may do our homework because it is fun in the early grades and mommy and/or daddy sits with us and gives us attention. Mastery of new skills (walking, reading, spelling) is also very motivating to us when young (DSI), making us feel "grown up." We may also do homework to keep us out of trouble (PSI) or to get praise from our parents (DSI). In the long run, we will get a sense of accomplishment from a chore like homework, which will outweigh the work involved. And then we feel good about ourselves. Instilling a good work ethic in a young child is an important gift that will last a lifetime.

Another valuable lesson that parents can teach is to delay DSI. We can't have dessert until after dinner, can't watch television or go out and play until our homework is completed and, eventually, can't enjoy the fruits of our labor until the work week is over. We learn to delay DSI by taking turns with, and sharing the TV remote with, our bratty brother. These lessons help us to manage and shape our own self-interest as we get older.

The temperaments we are born with, the rules that we are taught by parents and teachers combine with the rewards and consequences we receive for our actions, to shape our self-interest. A temperamentally nervous child and a fearless child may grow up in the same family under the same set of rules, but receive different consequences from parents and teachers. The nervous child may exhibit many PSI behaviors and never cross a line or stretch an envelope, in effect becoming a "goody two-shoes." The fearless one becomes a constant source of concern to parents and is thought of as a "wild child."

Our parents teach us to look out for ourselves directly as we grow up. We're told to "stick up for yourself" and not to let anyone "take advantage of you." We're told to "try hard" in whatever we do and we're encouraged to play to win. Overzealous parents at a little league game are an exaggerated version of this. If our strivings meet with success we're lucky, but sometimes if we lose often enough, we devalue the activity or stop playing entirely, as an obvious display of protective self-interest. Parents would be better off encouraging the effort and being pleased with whatever the result turned out to be. That way, PSI won't kick in as much or as often to make the child avoid the activity. If children learn that *participation* is fun in and of itself and *winning* is just icing on the cake, it is more likely that more children will *want* to participate.

The combination of PSI and DSI behaviors result in individual "comfort zones" in various venues. At home, we brush our teeth, say "Please" and "Thank You," and come home from playing on time. This gets us what we want (peace, rewards, smiles) and avoids what we don't want (to be criticized or punished). In school, we appear to pay attention, we dress a certain way (so as to be popular, or at least not to stand out) and are polite to our teachers. These behaviors are comfortable for us; they become "us." And, being self-interested, we seek to increase our comfort level, and/or decrease our discomfort.

Just as certain behaviors become "us," behaviors that we see as "not us" are seen as wrong or bad. Thus, a boy who dresses differently might be laughed at, or a girl who misbehaves in class may get a reputation for "always being in trouble."

THE TEEN YEARS

As we enter our teens, the authority figures who control and teach, the ones that channel our DSI and teach us PSI, have less oversight. We are alone more of the time, are allowed to play outside with peers and on our own. We are also growing in size and our DSI finds new wants and needs, involving some kind of fun. Some of it is healthy, some not.

Many DSI activities are misguided, in the sense that although they are fun and feel good at the time, they are not good for the individual in the long run. Included here are not doing homework, not paying attention in school, using alcohol, drugs, having sex at an early age, cutting school, etc.

We hope that by teaching PSI at earlier ages, as well as the appropriate channels for DSI, the budding teen will make less misguided choices when faced with novel (for them) situations. We "inoculate" them, hoping that when approached to use drugs or alcohol they will make the right decision, even if it means saying "no" to a peer.

We all have a need to fulfill our DSI, the only question is through which avenue. We can feel good about ourselves as a teen by being the kid that can get the most beer, is the best athlete, the most popular, the best musician, the sweetest/nicest, best behaved child, the best student etc., or any combination of the above. Parents start the channeling process by pointing kids in the right direction, but by teenage years all bets are off.

As teens, we know who the most attractive members of the opposite sex are and fantasize about them. If we can't have them for real, we can in our minds. Most of us dream of being movie or rock stars, star athletes or millionaires. We dream about dating the hottie, driving the fancy sports car, being famous or powerful. It is said that teens feel invincible, another fantasy that fulfills DSI but can lead us into trouble if we don't grow out of it. Teens getting speeding tickets and into accidents within months of obtaining their license makes the point. All of these fantasies may be little more than fulfilling DSI in an achievable and (mostly) harmless way.

What does that say about our mind set as we enter adult years. It would seem that we are self-interest machines (yes, "SIMs") as we prepare to enter the work force. Not unpredictably, the realm of work, money and economics is where the "outing" of ISI is the most obvious.

THE EARLY ADULT YEARS

By the time we reach our majority, the die is mostly cast. The way we express our self-interest has been established, buffered by years of development. We are all looking out for ourselves (ISI), but some of us exhibit more PSI than DSI and some more the other way around. We all vary in the amount of MSI we exhibit; i.e. some of us learn from our mistakes better than others. It would be interesting to scale PSI, DSI and MSI and look at the ratios among them, as well as correlate these indices with behaviors.

In effect the specific pattern of ways in which we seek to follow our ISI describe our kind of people we become. Some of us are athletic and play, follow and read about our sports. Others are "artsy," or "intellectual" or "geeky." We also vary in the way we approach other people. Some of us are insular and don't need much social interaction, having learned to fulfill our ISI in solitary activities. Others are social animals and are uncomfortable alone. Some of us, through innate personality and the consequences we get, become outgoing and assertive. Still others are meek and shy.

That is not to say that what satisfies our self-interest doesn't change over time. A 21 year old male may not want to marry or have children. By the time he hits thirty he may want to settle down with a partner and have kids. Twenty-somethings can be happy with a job that is "fun," but as we age, a career with a modicum of security and health insurance may take precedence. "Growing up" may just be the trading of some ways of sating self-interest for others.

Things that were taught to us when younger, such as the importance of a strong work ethic and the ability to delay DSI can predict success or failure in our careers and marriages. Those who can work hard are better providers, and those that can avoid procrastination and the lure of instant pleasure (sexual liaisons, overindulgence in substances, gambling) make better spouses and parents.

THE LATER ADULT YEARS

A recent injury gave me insight into how self-interest changes as we get older. The weights on the balance scale, between "do" and "don't do" changed. When in pain, I measured the walking distance of everything I did, even if it was just from the bedroom to the kitchen. My DSI didn't change; I still wanted to do the same things, but the cost of doing some of them became greater.

As people age they are less strong, feel more vulnerable, get overwhelmed more easily and learn new things with more difficulty. The thought of being away from the comforts of home, of taking a subway or plane trip, of doing a lot of walking or strenuous activity (such as cleaning up the basement or garage) or of learning a new skill (computer, internet use, or cell phone) becomes much less appealing. ISI becomes more PSI and less DSI, and activities yield to more sedentary pastimes (i.e. the ratio of PSI to DSI varies directly with age).

This may explain why older people spend time dwelling on the past. The "old days" were more pleasant than the limited life some older people lead. Certainly old times present more good memories than recent ones. Plus the fantasy/reminiscence is pleasant in and of itself, taking one away from the reality of being immobile or ill.

Withdrawal from life, by degrees, becomes more appealing than participation. You're retired for a while, don't have an identity, don't have much to contribute to the conversation and don't command much respect from youngsters (compared to when you were younger and more vital). Being ignored smarts and stings. The way you lived your life worked for you, yet seems irrelevant or uninteresting to younger people. You feel censured, which leads you to withdraw and avoid (PSI). Communities catering to seniors become more appealing on many levels.

Even some joyous family events, such as a wedding, can point out how much you *can't* do. You watch others dance and flit around the room as you sit there. And you realize that there is no going back. It won't get any better, and it will, eventually, get worse. So, just like some women who are past child-bearing years and are childless may avoid situations that involve children because it hurts, or some men that aren't wealthy are jealous of those that are, some seniors become a little bitter and envious.

Your ISI changes to include more PSI. It's not as if every young person will mug you, but you realize your helplessness. And, realistically, you know you could fall and break something in a heartbeat. The vulnerability is scary, so you stay in your comfort zone which may be limited to your own neighborhood or apartment, and stick with familiar doctors and stores. And you are very very cautious, which defines your new ISI. You focus on what you still *can* do that brings pleasure. You talk on the phone, you watch your favorite TV shows, you look at old pictures and, you reminisce.

Our life cycles, quite simply, involve being taught appropriate ways to channel our self-interest when we are young, and then, as we age, revising and re-revising these ways, making them appropriate to our current life situation.

Chapter 6: Self-Interest At The Family Level

Self-Interest is normal and mundane. It's not just greedy Wall Street executives, corporate moguls or even overenthusiastic surgeons whose lives are dictated by self-interest. It's all of us.

Take a hypothetical couple, Nick and Nora, who earn $100,000 between them. They have two children. Let's look at their joint checking account to see how their money is spent. See if you can find money spent that is *not* in their self-interest, one way or another.

Federal income tax	$15,000
State income tax/Social security	6,000
Mortgage/real estate tax	24,000
Utilities/phones	7,000
Home improvements/maintenance	5,000
Food	10,000
Car payments/gas/insurance	8,000
Health insurance (part contribution)	4,000
Clothing/adults and kids	2,500
Gifts/holidays and birthdays	2,500

Entertainment/vacations	6,000
Charity	2,000
Savings/retirement and college	6,000
Miscellaneous	3,000

The first thing we notice is that expenditures total $101,000, meaning that the couple is slowly building debt, like many of the rest of us. Okay, how are their expenditures distributed?

The first two categories, taxes and Social Security fees, are paid ($21,000 in total) so the couple can obey the law of the land and thus stay out of trouble. The philosopher Hegel would call these expenses "Universal Altruism," but Nick and Nora are not doing this out of the goodness of their hearts. They don't enjoy paying taxes, but they are brought up to be rule-obedient citizens. Besides, they have no choice since their employers dole out what's due from their paychecks before they see a dime.

They take a bit of comfort in knowing, rather hoping, that some day they will retire and enjoy their Social Security benefits. Note that this type of self-interest is a mixture of PSI and DSI. They feel somewhat proud that they are making it as a family (DSI) but also are loathe to cheat on their income taxes for fear of the IRS (PSI).

They pay the mortgage and repair their home, as well as keep up with the utility bills so that they can provide themselves and their children with a decent place to live (which costs $36,000). They hope that one day they will be able to afford more house, but living in a three bedroom, 1 1/2 bath ranch is fine for now.   Other necessities include food for the family, car expenses, which allows them to get to work to earn the money that so quickly slips between their fingers, contributing to the cost of medical insurance provided by Nora's employer, and clothing and gifts ($27,000).

They attend religious services locally and feel an obligation to support the institution with deductible charitable contributions ($2,000). For them, giving avoids guilt and, since they believe in God, provides a small down payment on their ticket to heaven and instills good values in their children. Savings for both their own retirement and their children's college educations gives them some peace of mind (at a cost of $6,000). They spend minor amounts for miscellaneous necessities or for the sake of expedience (taking an occasional taxi, buying a cup of coffee on the way to work, picking up a newspaper, getting a haircut).

Six percent, or $6,000, includes the fun stuff. Going out to eat and/or to the movies once per week, as well as a romantic weekend in the mountains for Nick and Nora, and a shore house rental during the summer for the whole family, all come out of this pile. Every last penny seems to be attributable to Nick's self-interest or Nora's self-interest, direct and/or protective, as long as we include the children's needs as their own. Even the two percent of their income given to charity makes Nick and Nora feel better, being a reciprocity for what they get out of going to church or as a feeling "that they've done the right thing" and have taught their children the right thing. Hypocrisy doesn't feel good. Self-interest, all the time.

Looking at the example of Nick and Nora, it seems that most ways of satisfying self-interest involve money. While there are exceptions, most seemingly non-monetary ways of chasing our wants somewhere along the way involves economic activity. We pay to be educated (either through taxes or through tuition), we pay to pray through dues or contributions to our preferred house of worship, we pay to eat, drive, play video games, take a vacation and listen to our iPod. It should not be surprising that some of the laws of economics apply to ways of satisfying self-interest (supply and demand, for example).

An economist and philosopher named Friedrich Von Hayek[48] taught that markets govern not just economic factors, but all human needs, through the medium of money. Supporting one's family, belonging to a house of worship, buying an automobile and purchasing food are all done with money. Self-interest dictates needs and wants. Needs and wants, through money, are governed by economics. That's why the term "Selfonomics," a combination of self-interest and economics, fits our subject matter well. Note that self-interest is not the same as selfishness. Taking care of ones family and buying a minivan are all examples of self-interest, but are not necessarily selfish. Self-interest is much broader. Also, Selfonomics includes more than just greed and direct self-interest. Protective self-interest, misguided self-interest, and their ratios and interplay also fall under the same umbrella.

In visiting Nick and Nora, it was apparent that they are ordinary people. It shouldn't surprise us that self-interest underlies their lives. After all those American colonists who were the best survivors and best competitors were the ones that wrote our Constitution. The same Constitution that established our Democracy, where we all get to vote our self-interest and work in a capitalist, survival of the fittest, economy. Anyone surprised? It should also not be a shock that a document that begins with "We the People" could be a blueprint of a society denoted by "Me the People."

---

[48] "The Use of Knowledge in Society." The American Economic Review, 1945.

CHAPTER 7: SELF-INTEREST FROM A PSYCHOLOGIST'S POINT OF VIEW

I am a psychologist by trade. Selfonomics theory, the belief that it's all self-interest, all the time, does an excellent job of describing, explaining and predicting the behavior of the people I counsel. And it certainly provides an interesting and novel way of looking at behavior. For example, what do the following behaviors have in common?

> Building up credit card debt
>
> Gambling excessively
>
> Substance abuse
>
> Overeating

In terms of ISI, the commonality is a person choosing to act in a way that favors their short-term self-interest (DSI) over their long-term self-interest. They want something now, get it, and pay for it later. The inability to delay gratification is easy to see as Misguided Self-Interest, or MSI. Note that *occasional* spending, gambling, drinking and overeating are not a problem. It is only when they are taken to excess that trouble ensues.

Procrastination and laziness are related, but involve PSI. When I put off a chore or avoid it altogether by procrastinating, I "protect" myself from hard work writing that term-paper or vacuuming the house, but pay for it with guilt and/or censure later on. As before, it is an inability to delay self-interest (PSI) to goof off in favor of acting in a way that favors one's long-term self-interest. Avoid the chore now, and pay for it later. As before, it is Misguided Self-Interest. Occasional acts of procrastination (sleeping in on a weekend day, taking a "mental health day" once a year, vacuuming Wednesday instead of Tuesday) are not a problem. In excess they are.

In contrast to the behaviors above, *delay* of gratification, be it delaying pleasure-seeking (DSI) or foregoing pain-avoidance (PSI), predicts success in life. People who put work before play and can enjoy their passions in moderation have a leg up in this world. Inability to delay either pleasure or the avoidance of pain (hard work) doesn't work quite so well.

As mentioned earlier, one of the first things that clued me in to the importance of self-interest was asking myself to try and figure out the motives of my patients. After getting feedback as to the accuracy of my guesses, I then made corrections to my own thinking based on what I was told. It turns out that my patients, in fact all of us, have patterns of self-interest. Some of these patterns are adaptive, in that they support mental "health," whatever that is, and others don't, creating the need to seek counseling.[49]

For example, we all have our individual self-interests working for us, but some of us have more DSI than PSI and some have the reverse. Some of us are classically "neurotic," in that we have a lot of fears. In the terminology presented here, our PSI dominates our DSI. An example is Carol, 28, who has an obsessive-compulsive style. Carol is very bright and politically savvy. She clips articles from periodicals for later reading, but never seems to get through the stacks that pile up on her coffee table. She can't throw them out until they are read, so her apartment is messy. She buys clothes, some of which fit and some of which don't, and need to be returned. They are in another pile, in another corner, and remain there forever. Carol hates her job, but never can find the time to look for another. She gets caught up in the minutiae of life, plowing ahead, but never getting anywhere. She second guesses every decision she makes, often getting paralyzed by the

---

[49] I believe that therapy or counseling is merely common sense and objectivity, guided by experience.

process, so that a choice never gets made. In self-interest terms, Carol is dominated by PSI, trying to avoid feeling bad by not making a mistake that she will regret. As a result, most of her life is characterized by inaction and self-flagellation.

Other patients don't have enough PSI and are dominated by their pleasure-seeking DSI. Josie met a guy with whom she had a lot in common, and fell in love. Hard. But John is a police officer and has many female friends. He's also somewhat outgoing and can be flirtatious. John was kind of geeky as a teenager and seems to be enthralled by the attention he gets from women now that he's no longer invisible. Josie takes John's attention to other women as disrespecting her. She needs to realize that it has nothing to do with her. John would do the same to Kathy, Betty or you, Josie.

He will only stop the flirting if it suits *his* needs. Perhaps if Josie is important enough to him, he will. In a way, Josie is irrelevant. He may not be ready to settle down yet. Or he may not care enough. There's nothing Josie can do. John will do what he perceives is in his own self-interest. You can't force him to want to be monogamous or to love you. You have to do what's in your own self-interest, which might mean moving on if he can't or won't change his ways.

Still others are a complicated mix of PSI and DSI. Jodi is 50 and recently divorced, having been cheated on by her ex-husband several times. Jodi was picked on as a child for being out of style, and didn't have many close friends. She is understandably nervous about men and has her defenses up (PSI). She is currently dating a nice man named Tom, and they get along famously (DSI). He is also divorced, and was cheated on by his wife. Jodi is deathly afraid of being dumped (PSI). She reports, however, that Tom seems to enjoy their time together, keeps calling and showing up on time, and is a stable and predictable person. Her fears (PSI) are overblown. Tom won't disappear (unless she drives him nuts by showing her insecurity), and not because he's doing *her* a favor. He's doing *himself* a favor (his own DSI). If she is accurately portraying the interactions, why would he dump her? He's not a masochist. The relationship works for *him*! He's staying with her because it *works* for him; she rings his bell.

The diagram below may help to visually describe the types of self-interest presented by a patient:[50]

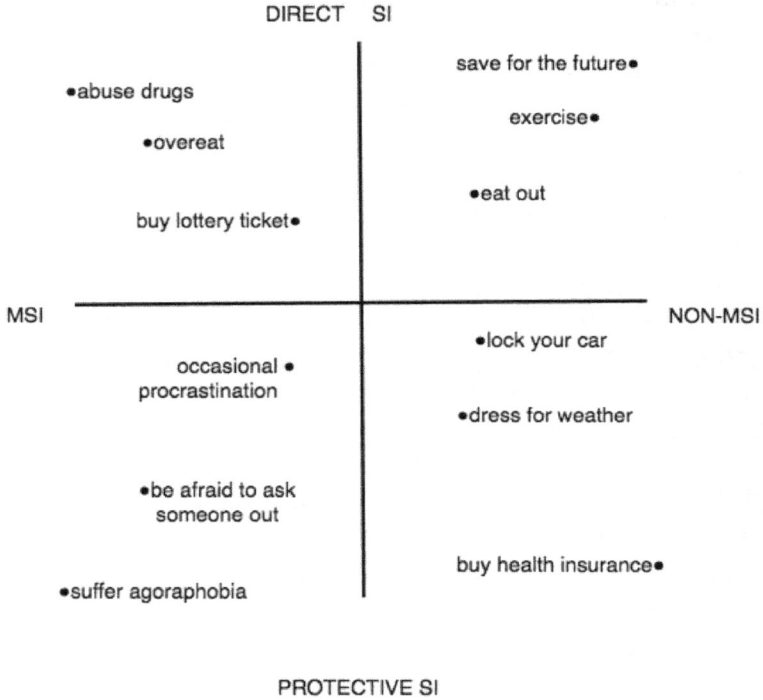

DIRECT SI

save for the future•

•abuse drugs

exercise•

•overeat

•eat out

buy lottery ticket•

MSI ——————————————————————— NON-MSI

•lock your car

occasional •
procrastination

•dress for weather

•be afraid to ask
someone out

buy health insurance•

•suffer agoraphobia

PROTECTIVE SI

The y-axis runs from DSI down to PSI, while the x-axis runs from MSI to self-interest that is not misguided. A person's emitted behaviors can be placed on the graph as a data point. For most of us, our data points will be distributed among all four quadrants. For some, the data

---

[50] Some caveats: a) within limits there are few rights and wrongs, b) misguided vs. non-misguided values may only be apparent after the fact, and c) it is expected that all people will exhibit behavior in all four quadrants.

may cluster in one or two of the quadrants. For example, someone who is anxiety-ridden, may exhibit behavior that falls only in the two lower quadrants; that is, they protect themselves at all costs, whether the behaviors are misguided or not. Someone who is a "daredevil" or a "sensation seeker"[51] [52] may exhibit behaviors in the top left quadrant; that is, they seek pleasure in misguided ways.

A third dimension could be added to this paradigm representing time. That way, behavioral choices over the life cycle may be viewed, or even from before therapy to after it. It is expected that for most of us, our behaviors will become more protective and less misguided as we get older.

While this is not a book on psychology alone, it is important to note how self-interest plays itself out in a therapeutic setting. It is believed that all behavior is motivated by the self-interest of the individual and that personality can be viewed as the way we learn (are taught) to channel that self-interest within, of course, the parameters set by our inherited biology. In most cases, this works well. For some people, the way they look out for themselves isn't working. Much of the way they fulfill their self-interest is misguided. They seek therapy to make things better. And it is in the best interest of the therapist, and indirectly the patient, to examine patterns of direct, protective and misguided self-interest and make them a central focus of therapy.

---

[51] This formulation brings to attention the seminal work of Marv Zuckerman in the field of "sensation seeking." See: Zuckerman, Marv. "Biological Bases of Sensation Seeking, Impulsivity and Anxiety." 1983, Erlbaum.

[52] See also an excellent summary article: Kopeikin, Hal S. "Sensation Seeking." http://www.psych.ucsb.edu/~kopeikin/sssinfo.htm.

CHAPTER 8: SELF-INTEREST AND MAKING DECISIONS

Earlier it was mentioned that people tend to behave in patterns. That is, they usually seek their ISI, DSI, PSI and MSI in habitual ways. While in general this is true, it's obvious that we all can change our minds at the drop of the hat, depending on the issue involved. One moment one choice serves our self-interest and then, poof, the next minute we make a different choice. Can Selfonomics theory account for this wavering? Yes.

Here's a situation I often pose to my patients. It's taken from a book I wrote at an earlier point in time:[53]

Let's say you drive a Toyota Camry. Good car, but six years old. Getting long in the tooth. Consider this hypothetical bonanza: Suppose someone would be willing to give you a brand new stripper (no, not that kind) Camry, which had no air conditioning, no CD player, no sunroof, no leather and, most important, no miles. ....OR you could choose a demonstrator Camry, one that has been driven by a salesman, prospective customers or both. This car has all the bells and whistles. It has a sunroof, leather, 6 CD changer, Bluetooth air conditioning, a GPS system which talks to you in your choice of voices; the works. The catch is that this one has 100,000 miles on it.

Under these conditions, most of us would opt for the stripped model, feeling that at 100K, the second car's days were numbered. When I give this example, if a client says they'd prefer the stripper, I'll say, "What about if the demo

---

[53] *You're Not Nuts... You've Just Got Issues. (2007)*. Outskirts Press.

had only 80K miles? If they hold to their preference, I'll reduce it to 60k miles and keep going.

At some point, all people will hesitate, then change their minds. For example they'll say "If it has 25,000 miles, I'll take the demo." I say, what about 26,000? They'll say, "okay." "How about 27K?" "No, I'd take the new one. How about 26,500? I do usually stop before they throw something at me, but the point has been made.

All of us have our "break even" or "tipping" points, the mileage at which taking the new stripped model is just about as desirable as taking the loaded demo. Put in terms of self-interest, at the break even point, the perceived ISI of one choice is equal to the perceived ISI of the other. You can almost see the wheels turning in the head of the decider... "more mileage, more repairs, less mileage, fewer breakdowns."

This verbal experiment may be a way of measuring whether a person has a style that favors either DSI or PSI. The stripped version with no miles is a defensive choice. It will promise years of maintenance free operation, little or no repairs and it will start in five degree weather. It is the choice of people who want to play it safe. The demo car appeals to the wild person in us. We see ourselves gliding along with the stereo blasting, sitting on comfy leather seats and the sun warming our pates through the sunroof. But since it has many miles, it is a riskier proposition. It is more a DSI choice. We posit that if one person's tipping point is 80.000 miles and another's is 30,000, that the latter would have more of a PSI style than the former. (Of course, we would have to control for certain variables such as age, gender and income level.)–

Note that this is a very simple situation. By manipulating just one variable, mileage, we can get someone to change what they think is in their best self-interest. Now what if we threw in other variables, such as price of the car, the mileage it gets, how large and fast it goes, etc. The only thing that we see, from the outside, is a binary choice; i.e. Car #1 or Car #2. What's going on inside for the decider is a flurry of pluses and minuses involving a myriad of variables.

An individual's perceived self-interest is not unidimensional and is not black or white. It is a mash-up of both positives and negatives along various dimensions, including the dimension of time. That is, I may reach different decisions at different stages of my life. Also note that in our example, at around 25,000 miles the two choices were virtually indistinguishable for our subject. And when we realize that the decision is a murky one, it is understandable how a person may change his/her mind in an instant.

Decisions that are 50-50 or close to it, such as the choice of car at roughly 25,000 miles, are difficult to make. Deciding what's in our ISI is easy when the decisions are 80-20. "Would you like some more mashed potatoes?" "No thanks, I'm full." 70-30 decisions are easy. "Should I take an umbrella?" "Sure, better safe than sorry." Even 60-40 decisions aren't too bad. "Want another cup of coffee?" "MMh, yeah, but I'd better not. I won't sleep. But thanks...." It's only the close ones that make us think a lot. Or ruminate. Or stall because we don't know what the *right* choice is for us. Well...the message here is that *there is no right choice.* Should you see movie A or movie B? Should you eat Italian or Mexican? Should you order a steak or the chicken? No correct choice. Doesn't it stand to reason that if there really *were* a correct choice, a right answer, that we'd all be driving the same car, eating the same food, wearing the same clothes and the movie theaters that show the one movie everyone wants to see would be way overcrowded? We'd all have the same ISIs.

All of us experience situations where the best option for us at the time is not clear, where the cost/benefit ratio seems equal for the various choices in front of us. What separates us is not whether one of us has *the* right answers for his or her life and someone else does not. The message here is that there *isn't one* right answer. So what differs among us is the ability or inability to see that the choices before us are just about the same in value, and our willingness (or unwillingness) to flip that coin.

Further, realizing that there is no right answer for us at the time helps us to avoid second guessing ourselves after the decision has been made. We realize that we did the best we could at making the decision, and the best we could do is...the best we can do. If you invest in stocks, you don't have to be right all the time. In fact, if you're right 52% of the time, you'll be way ahead of the game (that's how the casinos win...a tiny positive edge and lots of repetitions).

The car example was a choice between two good outcomes. Situations which offer choices between two bad outcomes are not so much fun, especially when they occur in real life. Suppose you're in a relationship. Not a good one, but a relationship nonetheless. Let's also assume, for the sake of the kids, that there are no kids. Kids complicate decisions.

Staying or going must be very close to a 50-50 decision. If it was much worse, you'd be gone. See ya. If it was much better, you'd stay and not think of leaving so often. Some days you lean towards staying, some days towards leaving. Depends on whether he or she "makes" you angry on a given day with a given action (the quotes remind us that we are the ones that control whether we get angry, or at least should be).

The situation we're now in is a poster child for "no win." The scale stays balanced. Well, why not leave? On the "stay" side it's mostly protective self-interest. A "bird in the hand..." type of thinking. He/she's not so bad; it's scary out there; who else will tolerate your idiosyncrasies or bad breath or paunch? At least you've got security here. The devil you know is better than the devil you don't know. So you stay, and remain unhappy. Could the situation get much worse? On the "go" side are both Direct Self-Interest and PSI arguments. I could be so much happier being single or with someone else. But I'll be poorer, and alone, and I'll lose my friends...

If you're not willing to flip a coin in this situation, and many of us would not be, then the only thing you can control is to work on changing the weights on one or the other sides of the scale. For example, you can go back to school so you can earn more money and support yourself. You can lose weight, exercise, preen yourself or actually brush your teeth to make yourself more appealing to others should you eventually choose to go. These efforts will give you more currency, literally and figuratively if you choose to become single. They will also help the way you feel about yourself and might even make your significant other think that maybe he or she doesn't want to lose you without a fight.

You could also put your cards on the table with your partner. "I'm not real happy with our relationship. My guess is that you're not either. We have to make it better or move on. We both deserve better, and life's too short." This is where concessions come in, hopefully on both parts. "I'll stop doing this, if you'll stop doing that." Or suggesting that you look for outside help from a counselor so at least you can both say you tried. Living in a mediocre relationship is not such a great idea. But look at the bright side. At least the years of your life will go by much more slowly than they would if you were enjoying yourself.

The variable of time also affects what we see as in our individual self-interest. When we are in our thirties we work hard, foregoing leisure time and recreational activities, to make our mark in the world; to acquire things like a new or bigger house and a new car. Thirty years later, after we've lived in the house and driven new cars, we realize that "things" are nice to have, but aren't everything in life. The lure of those things gets old as we do. We want to experience life while we still can. At thirty-five the scale was tilted towards hard work and sacrifice and chasing DSI pursuits. At sixty-five the scale tilts towards less work and smelling whatever roses we can still smell. We also grow more cautious in our investments, activities and behaviors, which involve more PSI than DSI. So a decision that was in our ISI at thirty-five may be less important for our ISI at sixty-five.

Mass, fairly rapid shifts in self-interest can affect society in a big way. "Paradigm shift" is a term suggested by Thomas Kuhn,[54] a philosopher of science, in 1972. Kuhn proposed the term to describe significant changes in scientific thought, as when heliocentrism replaced geocentrism, or when Einstein developed the theory of relativity which replaced prior thinking about the nature of physics. After Kuhn, other theorists have used the term to describe the rapid change in thinking when the printing press was invented or when the internet came into widespread use. In general usage, it refers to any widespread change in thought patterns. Kuhn's paradigms were not limited to major changes, but are often interpreted that way. A paradigm could be a smaller but signal change such as the discovery of the double helix structure of DNA. This forever altered the way we think, but did not replace another theory. What changes for us is that we realize, individually, that the old way of thinking is inferior to the new way. Not wanting to be left behind, we all jump on the bandwagon. It serves our ISI to do so.

A rapid shift in the behavior of millions followed changing laws which allowed non-smokers to express their ISI. Prior to roughly 1980, smokers had all the rights. Smoking was allowed at work, in college classrooms, at social gatherings, in restaurants and at home. Places that forbade smoking were few and far between. Hospitals come to mind, although most waiting rooms still allowed it. If a person was adversely affected by smoke, it was *their* responsibility to avoid being in rooms with smokers. Few people would ask a smoker to "put it out." Within a period of roughly ten to twenty years, the tide changed drastically.

Led by research on second-hand smoke, and the resultant policy decisions to ban smoking in public places,

---

[54] Kuhn, T. (1962). *The Structure of Scientific Revolutions.* Univ. of Chicago Press.

by the year 2000, non-smokers had reclaimed their breathing environments. Smoking was forbidden in most office spaces, restaurants and at most social events. The smoker was the one that had to adapt, either by staying away from an indoor location, or by taking a break outside to have a smoke. The shift from smokers' to nonsmokers' rights represents a fairly rapid paradigm shift, at least in America. The great majority of Americans, even if they still smoke, accept the fact that they cannot befoul the air that others breathe. They accept their second-class citizenry. Non-smokers probably never enjoyed being deluged with smoke, but the laws allowed it. When the laws changed, people felt empowered to express their individual self-interests by telling a smoker to go outside.

This paradigm shift helped to reduce the percentage of people that smoke, as did the increasing price of a pack of cigarettes. Smoking became more difficult to do because working in a non-smoking environment created urges to smoke that were not easily sated. Most people, even family members, became more negative and vocal about the smoker's habit. In effect, the weights (costs and rewards) on the balance scale for the smoke-non-smoke decision changed. For many, this tipped the scale from "smoke" to "don't smoke." And once that decision was made, it became, in effect, a paradigm shift for the individual smoker. In fact any decision to quit an addiction, may be seen as a paradigm shift for the person making it (assuming they stick to the new decision to give up the habit).

It is likely that the decision to "go green" or to "reduce one's carbon footprint" will follow the same pattern. People have been talking about "global warming" for many years and the desire to reduce our dependence on foreign oil has been discussed since the first oil embargo in the 1970s. Nothing much changed however, until Al Gore and the IPCC (Intergovernmental Panel on Climate Change)[55]

---

[55] http://www.ipcc.ch

reports stirred the pot. The real kicker though, is not Mr. Gore's appeal to us, but our own selfish need to keep a tight grip on our own money. When gas prices rise, SUVs may become as welcome as smoke-filled rooms. Car companies almost had to give them away. Four dollar a gallon gas in the summer of 2008 is what sealed the deal for many Americans (although by the late fall of 2008 the price of gas had retreated to under two dollars, only to rise again to the same level in the Spring of 2011). It has changed the weights on the balance scale from "buy a big car" to "buy a small one." From not caring about how much we drive to measuring every trip in our heads in terms of how much money it will cost in gas.

As of this writing, the paradigm shift is just beginning, but it is not unreasonable to expect that in ten years, many people will make very different decisions about the size of the cars (and the size and energy efficiency of the homes) they buy and the travel distance to the jobs they take. We will become a greener society based on a shift in the weights on our personal balance scales. We may individually undergo a paradigm shift which will, added up over millions of people, change our society and our world. (It's not something we can count on, just yet. We Americans have short memories, as we learned after the oil embargo of the 1970s, after which the SUV made a mighty comeback.)

It is interesting that a paradigm shift of this kind implies that humans may have much in common with insects. "Swarm intelligence" is the study of how simple individual entities, without centralized leadership, taken in the aggregate, can mimic complex behavioral systems. A cardinal example can be found in ant colonies, in which without leadership, but guided by instinctual deposits of chemical compounds, ants perform complex "social" functions.[56]

As for humans, an example of swarm intelligence occurs when an un-coerced individual in a crowd, who starts clapping at a concert, leads others in the audience to start clapping, resulting in widespread applause. One person claps. Others, who also appreciated the performance but were too inhibited to start the clapping, soon follow suit. Then a critical mass is reached and many people who really didn't want to clap end up clapping so as to not stand out in the crowd. The occurrence of "The Wave" at a stadium event is another example. Thus individual decision making, summed over people over time, can result in (seemingly) concerted group action. Self-interest for the individual equates to the instinct-driven behavior of ants. The previous discussion of smokers' rights disappearing over a relatively short period of time fits this paradigm. And, presumably, individuals guided by self-interest, may be a prime mover in an inexorable march toward less carbon use.

To summarize, an individual's perceived self-interest is not unidimensional and is not black or white. It is a mash-up of both positives and negatives along various dimensions, including the dimension of time. Different decisions may be reached at different times, especially the closer the choices are to 50-50. With more than two choices, things become even more complicated. Decisions are made based on a combination of PSI and DSI. In other words, we decide based on what we see as being good for us and avoiding things that we think are bad for us.

---

[56] Bonabeau, Eric, Dorigo, Marco & Theraulaz, Guy. "Swarm Intelligence: From Natural to Artificial Studies," New York: Oxford University Press, 1999. Proceedings of the Santa Fe Institute Studies in the Sciences of Complexity.

CHAPTER 9: SELF-INTEREST, DISAGREEMENTS AND ARGUMENTS

Disagreements between or among people can be seen as a conflict between or among the self-interests of the parties involved, be they individuals or groups. Looked at this way, certain general rules can be deduced which may aid in the understanding of these conflicts. Consider the following anecdote:

> I was walking by a carnival the other day and saw a sign for a fortune teller. The sign said "Wanda Knows All." Sounded interesting, so I went in. Her services didn't come cheap (five bucks, if you must know), but I figured since I was paying her, she would be somewhat obligated to say nice things about me. That turned out to be a bad assumption. I asked her to describe the kind of person she thought I was. This is what Wanda said to me:

> "You're a guy who thinks logically most of the time, even though you *think* you think logically *all* of the time. You got most of your beliefs that you hold from your parents when you were young. You've tweaked a few of them by learning from experience and those appeal to you more because you feel "ownership" of them. But I see that almost all of those beliefs are quite resistant to change.
> You are only good at controlling your own behavior, although you waste a lot of time trying

to change the behavior of others and get frustrated when it doesn't work. You want to win in sports and excel at school regardless of whether or not you have the talent to do so. Knowing that you tried your best provides little comfort for you. As an adult you even end up avoiding situations in which you are not successful (that's why you quit the bowling league and refuse to play Scrabble any more). It's obvious that you have trouble accepting failure.

You always follow your own self-interest. You choose friends, dates and activities based on what's good for *you*. You only do good deeds to feel virtuous about yourself, to reduce guilt or fear, or to get love from someone you want it from. You care about Planet Earth only if it will save you a buck."

Boy, was I insulted! How could Wanda say those cruel things about me? If I were really like that, I'd be a miserable human being, wouldn't I? And I'd probably get into all kinds of disagreements and arguments...

Given the assumption that all people are logical as well as looking out for their own self-interest, it should come as no surprise that there are disagreements. Let's consider a two-person situation and see what we can deduce. Think about the last time you had an argument with someone. Say your spouse or significant other. Did you think you were right? Do bears poop in the woods? Of course you did! Why would you argue unless you were right? Well, unbeknownst to you, about five minutes ago, I spoke with your spouse and they said that *they* were right. Not only that, but they said that *you* started the argument! What do you think of that, huh?

Is this possible? I don't mean is it possible that you were wrong. You probably were. But is it possible that both people think that they're right? Of course. Else why would they bother arguing? Imagine the following dialog:

> World-Weary Hardworking Hubby: Hi honey, I'm home.
>
> Harried Chore-Juggling Wife: Hi. (Then silence)
>
> WHH: (voice slightly elevated, interpreting her silence for her being out of hearing range): What's for dinner?
>
> HCW: I have no idea. I haven't had time to even think about it.
>
> WHH: (shaking his head in a disgruntled fashion): Man, I'm starved. Whaddya mean you haven't even thought about it. Tonight's Thursday. We usually have spaghetti.
>
> HCW: (her voice assuming a higher, more emotional pitch): I don't even know what day it is. Mary had unicycle practice and Johnny had to be driven to his kazoo lesson. And that's aside from doing the laundry and running errands. *You* put dinner up, if you want something to eat.
>
> WHH: (puffing up indignantly): C'mon, this is the third time this week I've had to scratch to find something to eat. I shouldn't have to beg to be fed. It's your *job* to put some kind of dinner on the table. Not just for me, but for the kids too!
>
> HCW: (losing it): Don't tell me what my job is. My job is surviving! I haven't had a minute to myself the whole day! (Stomps off to the bedroom, slams the door behind her.)

WHH: (walking to within five feet of the bedroom door and yelling to make sure she hears him): You know, when you act like this you sound just like your mother! (Turns to walk away.)

At this point, the bedroom door opens briefly, allowing an accurately thrown rolling pin to fly through the opening, towards and upside the head of WHH. The door slams shut again, we hear a thud and....silence.

Granted, the scenario was a little melodramatic, but most of us have been there with someone, at some time, minus the rolling pin. Which one of them was right? Was it the wife who was frazzled because despite being pulled in all directions by the kids and the chores, she received no consideration, empathy or support from her no-account husband? Or was it the husband, who toils long and hard only to be denied, on an all too regular basis, the sustenance he requires to keep on keepin' on? Was it the wife, exerting PSI, in effect saying to her husband, "I'm exhausted. Get lost!"? Or the husband, with his DSI of "I'm hungry. Feed me!"?

Before answering the question, who *started* the argument? The husband, by being impatient and condescending in his tone? Or the wife, by putting him last on her list and not having cooked dinner? Or perhaps the husband again, by invoking the specter of his mother-in-law (never a really great strategy)? Or the wife by raising her voice, stomping off and slamming the bedroom door, or throwing a strike to the head of her devoted life partner?

And, by the way, *when* did the argument begin? Was it when the husband walked into the house and acted in an impatient and demanding manner? Or when the wife raised her voice? Or when he invoked the dreaded mother-in-law? Or, perhaps, on Monday, the first day that dinner wasn't prepared because the wife had to take Johnny to Kazoos 'R' Us?

By now you've probably guessed that there's more than one answer to all of the above questions. As a matter of fact, the following statement is about as close as you're gonna get to a hard and fast rule in this book:

WHEN TWO PEOPLE ARGUE, THEY BOTH THINK THEY'RE RIGHT, THEY BOTH THINK THE OTHER ONE STARTED IT, AND THEY EACH THINK IT STARTED AT A DIFFERENT TIME!

(When you think about it, why else would they argue?)

Okay, you ask, how can they both be right? That one's easy, and is part of the above rule:

THEY BOTH ARE RIGHT, BECAUSE THEY'RE TALKING ABOUT DIFFERENT THINGS!

He's upset because the deal is that he goes out of the house to bring home the bacon, and she works in the house and cooks it. And he's right! There is no dinner, and that breaks an unstated agreement. She's upset because another unstated agreement is that spouses show each other consideration and help each other out when they're stressed, and he did neither. She's right. He *was* inconsiderate.   And if this makes sense, that both participants can be right for different reasons, then it also stands to reason that they each think the other started it (by breaking some kind of spoken or unspoken rule of the house) and that it started at a different time.

The same paradigms also come into play in squabbles between sects, religions and nations. Two countries, represented by their heads of state, have the interests of their respective citizens at heart. They are, in effect, looking out for the Group Self-Interest of their countrymen. Logically, they can both deduce that they've been wronged by their opposite number. According to the theory presented here, they *were* wronged by the other guy. So they *are* both right. This is possible because they're talking about different actions or insults which occurred at different points in time. And they *both* are sure that the other side started the conflict. One doesn't have to look very deep into the history books to find conflicts which cross generations and fit this model (China-Taiwan, Israelis-Palestinians, Northern Ireland, Hutus-Tootsies, Yankees-Red Sox fans, India-Pakistan, etc.). What follows is a generic facetious look at a potential conflict between nations.

Few people were aware of this, but recently the heads of two neighboring rival states met at a undisclosed location. We were privileged to be the proverbial "fly on the wall." The meeting was between the First Leading Eminent Minister (FLEM) of the People's Republic of Outer Neptunia (PROON) and the Prime Ulterior Satrap (PUS) of the Democratic Republic of Northern Estrangia (DRONE). Their dialogue follows:

FLEM of PROON: Hello, Satrap. I have asked you here to discuss the crisis that has developed in the border region between our two countries.

PUS of DRONE: Yes, Minister. It has become increasingly tense. It might improve dramatically if you would allow our workers to cross your border to work. There are jobs available in your country, and by closing the border you have left us without means to earn our daily bread.

FLEM of PROON: Satrap, you are aware that when we have allowed your workers to cross in the past, a high percentage of them stayed on in our country and weighed down our social services. We cannot afford to let them cross.

PUS of DRONE: You know, Minister, that during the first Estrangian Civil War, our infrastructure was damaged and we have not been able to recover since. Further, the PROONian politicians at the time funneled money to both sides of the conflict, making it last for twenty years and severely damaging our industries. Thus PROONians bear some responsibility for the plight of our people.

FLEM of PROON: I understand your position, Satrap, but Estrangian Civil Wars are not our business. The attempted assassination of our Grand Poopah Cyril in 1858 by a naturalized DRONEian citizen did nothing to lead us to want to be friendly to your country.

PUS of DRONE: That man was a PROONian, masquerading as a DRONEian! How dare you bring that controversy up again! I beseech you to take back what you said, forthwith!

FLEM of PROON: Never, dog-breath! (They both draw their swords.)

The rules are the same for representatives of nations as they are for spouses. Both the FLEM and the PUS are thinking logically and are acting in the Group Self-Interest of their respective citizens. They obviously each think that they are right (one side wants its workers to be able to cross the border to work, while the other resents having to pay for health and education services to those workers who don't return home), both think that the other country started the conflict (one points to the other as fomenting civil war while the other points to the attempted assassination of a previous leader) and both point to different points in time when the conflict began. All this can be true because they are talking about different things. And, as everybody knows, what is good for a PROONian is not necessarily good for a DRONEian.

Another possible roadblock to communication is that each message contains two parts: the content of said communication and the way (both verbal and non-verbal) it is delivered. When we are talking, we are focusing in on what we are saying, i.e. the content of our message, and not so much on the way we deliver it. The recipient of the message, on the other hand, is likely to focus on the *way* your message came across more than what you are actually saying. So that "You forgot to cook dinner, again!" will get the response "Don't yell at me. I'm not your slave!"

On the level of nations, some leaders have the reputation for being diplomatic in the way they deliver messages, while others are seen as bullies because of their abrasive styles. One can be certain if there is mistrust between two nations, that one nation will pay very close attention to the verbiage put out by the other side and interpret it in a negative way. And, as always in these disagreements, it's a two-way street.

A summary of the literature on social perception, sheds some light on why people disagree.[57] "In short, we

---

[57] Pronin, Emily, et. al. "How We See Ourselves and How We See Others," Science, vol. 320, p. 1177-1180 (5/302008).

judge others based on what we see, but ourselves based on what we think and feel." If we are acutely aware of our own thoughts and feelings, but have no idea about what someone else is thinking and feeling, we end up judging the other by their behavior. This may or may not reflect true intentions, but often we ascribe intentions to another, such as malice and greed. This leads to habits such as being blind to our own biases (but we see the biases of others quite clearly), projecting our own thoughts onto others, and tending to see others as unfair. We need to understand the difference between intention and behavior, both in others and in ourselves. This is similar to the assertion that behavior is observable, but self-interest is not. We don't know what's going on in the other person's head, or what his ISI will lead him to do. We can only get at his motives *inductively*.

Two people can't agree on everything, if only because they enter any given situation with a different set of premises and beliefs. And each person's beliefs are "steeled" by confirmation bias[58] over the years. In the first year of marriage, newlyweds can argue about whether toilet paper should be rolled over or under, about whether they do the dishes immediately after dinner or at some later time, who is responsible for cleaning the toilet, as well as

---

[58] **Confirmation bias** (also called **confirmatory bias** or **myside bias**) is the tendency of people to favor information that confirms their beliefs or hypotheses. People display this bias when they gather or remember information selectively, or when they interpret it in a biased way. The effect is stronger for emotionally charged issues and for deeply entrenched beliefs. People also tend to interpret ambiguous evidence as supporting their existing position. Biased search, interpretation and memory have been invoked to explain attitude polarization (when a disagreement becomes more extreme even though the different parties are exposed to the same evidence), belief perseverance (when beliefs persist after the evidence for them is shown to be false), the irrational primacy effect (a greater reliance on information encountered early in a series) and illusory correlation (when people falsely perceive an association between two events or situations). (http://en.wikipedia.org/wiki/Confirmation_bias)

more important things. Assuming the couple resolves these difference, their beliefs become more similar (i.e. they develop their own agreed-upon rules for behavior) or they have resigned themselves to "agree to disagree."

And we can never forget the "pride" factor. If I have a certain belief, I own it, and accepting a different opinion may be experienced by me as a "loss." It *feels like* I'm backing down or giving in. If both people in a relationship can admit error, then it is easier for the other to do the same. If one is stubborn or prideful, or some combination thereof, the second party will either catch on and not give in either, or give in regularly to avoid argument, thus establishing a dominant-submissive type of relationship. When one party is "never wrong," the best the other can do is learn to say, "to each to his own," or "let's agree to disagree."

Part III: Self-interest as an Explanatory Tool

Making the case that self-interest operates in all of us, all the time, creates some initial discomfort. After all, are we comparable to other members of the animal kingdom, or does being human put us "above it all." Are we that selfish that we will always put our needs before the needs of others? What about the "Golden Rule" or altruism? And what about the American Dream which implies that everyone can and should prosper? Let's look at these topics one at a time to see if they are consistent with Selfonomics theory.

Chapter 10: Self-interest and the Golden Rule

If we all pursue our ISI all the time, won't we get into a lot of fights and arguments? I mean, there are a whole host of situations in which what's good for you is bad for me, and vice versa. If you're wealthy and get a tax break that I can't use, aren't I losing to your benefit? If I beat you at tennis, won't you be resentful? If my wife spends money on clothes doesn't that mean that there will be less money available for me to spend on golf? There are various ways around these problems, but they all involve something titled the "Ethic of Reciprocity," also commonly called the "Golden Rule."

The Golden Rule is usually stated as, "Do unto others as you would have them do unto you." It's found in all cultures going back through recorded history and is the basis of human rights, ethics and laws governing virtually every society. Its converse is "Don't do unto others what you would not want done to you." The fact that it has been a part of humanity for so long carries the implication that it has always been known that self-interest must be kept in check, or that rampant, unregulated self-interest is not a good thing. And though the universality and centrality of self-interest is implied by the existence of the Golden Rule self-interest, as a separate term, is never mentioned.

What the Rule implies is that we are trading self-interest for self-interest. If we want something that is good for us, we have to be willing to do something that is good for another. If we want to avoid being hurt, we should not hurt others. The important concept is "trading." We can't have everything we want every time we want it. We can get now and give later. Or we can give now, and get later. The giving and the getting is reciprocal.

The Golden Rule is drilled into us starting at a very early age. I'll be nice to you, but I expect the same in return. If I am not treated nicely in return, I'll resent you. At some point, in the interest of my PSI, I may end the friendship. Note that although the Golden Rule says that we should do good things, it also implies a need to have regard for our own self-interest. In other words, figure out how you would want others to act toward you, and then treat them the same way. You have to know what *you* want first. It's not as selfless as it seems. It also implies a kind of empathy, like what Adam Smith referred to as sympathy for another person.[59]

The Golden Rule, also implies compromise, wherein each party gets a little bit of what they want, but not everything. When one starts from assumptions that all people think logically holding different beliefs and premises, and that we are all guided by self-interest, then people, groups and nations may very well be in competition for available resources. When disagreements arise, disputants must first accept that to disagree is normal because of differing beliefs, and that attempts at resolving those disagreements are not only noble, but expected and obligatory.

This follows logically from the knowledge that you are not always right or rather, that you are right and so is the other person (or nation). If we accept that both of us are correct for different reasons, and that we don't have to win all the time, then both sides can see the need to negotiate and compromise. Below are four methods of compromise, each slightly different, using disagreements between people and/or groups of people as examples.

1) **AVERAGING**: Some disagreements occur on variables, such as time and money, which

---

[59] Altman, Morris, ed. (2006). Handbook of Contemporary Behavioral Economics: Foundations and Developments. Armonk, N.Y.: M.E. Sharpe, Inc.

can be scaled, and thus averaged. If one spouse wants to spend $2000 on this year's family vacation and the other spouse thinks the family can only afford $1000, then $1500 would be a compromise. If one friend wants to meet at 7:00 p.m. and the other at 8:00 p.m., a solution is to meet at 7:30 p.m. Note that the arrived-at number does not have to lie directly in the middle. If one friend cannot get out of work early, the meeting time could be set at 7:45 p.m. Though not in the middle, it does concede something to both participants in the disagreement. This makes for good will, allows both sides to "save face" and discomfits and benefits both sides.

In a wider arena, if the leaders of one major particular party wants to dedicate x billion dollars to a particular national program, and the leaders of the other major party want to spend y billions, numbers between x and y represent compromises. Often the U.S. Senate and House of Representatives craft and pass similar bills that differ in the amount of funding and compromise in those amounts are necessary to allow passage.

2) **VETO POWER:** Generally, if I like choice A and you prefer B, we have reciprocal veto power over each other's choices and must look for C, a choice we both can live with. A husband likes Colonial furniture, his wife likes Danish Modern. Each vetoes the other's choice and they must look for a third style that they both agree on, say French Provincial. One spouse wants a four-door sports car, the other wants a minivan for the family. The compromise might be, after cross-vetoes, a "crossover" vehicle or station wagon.

You dislike Mexican food, I hate Chinese food, so we eat Italian or at a burger joint, or at a diner where each of us can find something we like.

Veto power is an integral part of the negotiating process at the United Nations. Members of the Security Council may veto each others Declarations, usually based on political beliefs. Knowing that a proposed Declaration faces possible veto leads to interesting posturing. A country may propose something to make a point even knowing that it will be vetoed, or the language of a proposal may be nuanced in such a manner meant to avoid a veto or reduce controversy.

In the United States, the President has veto power over bills passed by Congress and presented to him. Conversely, Congress can "veto the veto" by overriding the President's veto with a two-thirds vote by both Houses of Congress. With the growing power of China, India and the European Union, *de facto* veto power exists if one of these entities chooses not to go along with a global accord. The U.S. shunning the Kyoto Accords is an example. By not joining we, in effect, vetoed any significant coordinated policy towards global warming since we consume such a large part of the Earth's resources.

3) **ALTERNATION OF REALMS:** Both parties trade off so that each has a constant area of control. One spouse hates yard work while the other hates doing the laundry. The yard-hater does the laundry and the laundry-hater tends to the yard. Or one does the "inside work" while the other takes care of anything outside. Or one takes the responsibility of arranging social plans with friends and family, while the other takes care of the finances (paying bills, investing, budgeting). That's not to say that the social director should not have input to financial

decisions or the accountant can't express preferences for who the couple sees on Saturday night, but each realm has a "Captain" or leader.

Most governments divide power. In the U.S. we have three branches of government, each with its own purview. The President assigns cabinet positions, in effect, defining areas of turf for the various appointees. The C.I.A. has its portfolio, as does the Department of Interior, State, Treasury, etc. Other countries have their own territorial arrangements (e.g. Great Britain has the House of Lords, the House of Commons, M.I.5, etc.)

4) **ALTERNATION OF CHOICES WITHIN REALMS:** I like Mexican food, you like Chinese food. We alternate choices, so that this week the choice is mine, next week yours. Same with movies, either in theaters or with rentals. One week it's Clint Eastwood, the next it's Meryl Streep. If one of us tends to always pick movies that the other can't abide, such as violent films, we may be better off with strategy b) above, where we both have a veto.

At the United Nations, smaller nations rotate chances to sit on the Security Council. The sites for both Winter and Summer Olympics rotate between countries, as do the sites for other international meetings. Countries that can play nicely together by taking turns are seen as cooperative.

All four of these strategies, if used, leave the participants feeling good about each other and feeling as though they make a good "team." Each also saves face, if the results of the compromise are visible to others. Both sides get something, though not all of what they wanted. And a successful compromise sets a good precedent for future situations where the parties disagree. The need to trade and compromise our self-interest is taught to us early in our lives in the form of the Golden Rule. And the Golden Rule provides a roadmap to negotiating the self-interests of disparate parties.

Chapter 11: Accounting for Altruism

Selfonomics, which posits all self-interest, all the time, has to account for altruism and other acts of apparent benevolence and charity. Altruism, derived from a French word for "other people," is the antithesis of self-interest, meaning selflessness, or unselfish concern for the welfare of other people.

Selfonomics maintains that ordinary social interactions seem to be a result of us following our self-interest (seeking golf partners, dating), delaying self-interest (giving first, with payback later, a la the Golden Rule), or trading self-interest[60] (compromising, cooperating). An important difference between Selfonomics and other theories of psychological,[61] ethical or rational egoism,[62] is that the former posits different types of self-interest besides that which brings direct pleasure (protective and misguided self-interest).

---

[60] This has also been called "reciprocal altruism." See, for example, Lichtenberg, Judith. "Is Pure Altruism Possible?" New York Times, Opinionator, October 19, 2010.

[61] "Psychological egoism claims that each person has but one ultimate aim: her own welfare. This allows for action that fails to maximize perceived self-interest, but rules out the sort of behavior psychological egoists like to target — such as altruistic behavior or motivation by thoughts of duty alone. It allows for weakness of will, since in weakness of will cases I am still aiming at my own welfare; I am weak in that I do not act as I aim. And it allows for aiming at things other than one's welfare, such as helping others, where these things are a means to one's welfare." From the Stanford Encyclopedia of Philosophy, at http://plato.stanford.edu/entries/egoism/

[62] See, for example, the Wikipedia entry for "ethical egoism."

We are also distinguishing between *altruism* and altruistic *acts*. Altruistic acts are observable; giving to charity, helping a neighbor, visiting a sick loved one. Altruism is not. It is in the mind of the altruactor (just made up that word) and Selfonomics presumes that there is a reason that the act was performed that in some way benefits the actor. We may not know exactly what the motivation is, but we can make educated guesses through inductive reasoning, as described in an earlier chapter.

As an example, suppose you go to the post office and are five feet in front of a person who is behind you. Do you hold the door open for him? Of course. What if you are 100 feet ahead of them? Probably not. How about 25 feet? Or if the person is old or seems to be having trouble walking? If you hold the door open you a) have avoided being seen as rude by *not* holding it open and b) almost surely get a "thank you" which feels good. Both a) and b) serve your self-interest, even though, on the surface, you've just performed an altruistic act. If you chose *not* to hold the door open, there would be some shame or guilt attached, because you felt that you did not act well and were somewhat impolite. My guess is that most of us have felt this way on occasion, and haven't liked the feeling. Knowing this uncomfortable feeling will keep most of us holding open doors whenever possible. It is not out of altruism, but out of shame/guilt avoidance.[63]

We're far from the only ones questioning the existence of altruism. James Andreoni studied donations, and coined the term "warm glow altruism" to describe the good feeling that a person gets from giving. He pointed to "social pressure, guilt or sympathy as other possible motivators," which are other kinds of "impure" altruism.[64] David Leonhardt examined a body of research dealing with

---

[63] We might call this "incidental altruism."

[64] Andreoni, James. "Impure Altruism and Donations to Public Goods: A Theory of Warm-Glow Giving?" The Economic Journal, 1990, p. 464-77.

philanthropy. "Why do people give? Is it really to make the world a better place, to give back to the community as a token of gratitude? Or is giving instead about something less grand, like seeing your name on a building, responding to peer pressure or simply feeling good about yourself?"[65] The takeaway is that the act of giving is as much about the giver as it is about the gift or the cause. Nicholas D. Kristof reaches the same conclusion in a discussion of what makes us happy. "...it's difficult for humans to be truly selfless, for generosity feels so good."[66] This is supported by the research of neuroscientists, who find that charitable acts trigger the same kind of brain activity as does food and sex.[67]

Recent research has centered around the supposition that altruistic behavior has been honed through natural selection, beginning with the need of hunter-gatherer societies to pool resources in order to bring down large game or pick edible berries and nuts. The need to cooperate, passed down over the millennia, has led to the existence of observed altruistic actions that is not seen in other species.[68][69]

Through the lens of the infamous Kitty Genovese murder of 1964, Levitt and Dubner took a look at altruism. In both real life situations and classroom experiments, the authors find that altruism seems to disappear into thin air. Good acts are explainable in terms of fears of rejection,

---

[65] Leonhardt, David. "What Makes People Give?" New York Times, March 9, 2008.

[66] Kristof, Nicholas D. "Our Basic Human Pleasures: Food, Sex and Giving," New York Times, January 16, 2010.

[67] Vedantam, Shankar. "If It Feels Good To Be Good, It Might Be Only Natural." Washington Post, May 28, 2007.

[68] Wade, Nicholas. "We May Be Born With An Urge To Help." New York Times, November 30, 2009.

[69] Dawkins, Richard. op. cit.

retribution and scrutiny as well as a desire to protect one's reputation. They conclude, "Most giving is, as economists call it, *impure altruism* or *warm-glow altruism.* You give not only because you want to help but because it makes you look good, or feel good, or perhaps feel less bad."[70]

Levitt and Dubner stop short of a categorical statement such as "All giving is..." and don't generalize to state that all of these alternate explanations have in common that they serve an individual's self-interest. They mention several times, "*Homo economicus*, that hyper-rational, self-interested creature that dismal scientists had embraced since the beginning of time..." and posit a *homo altruisticus*, which they then disprove. The truth may be closer to *homo selfonomicus*. Levitt and Dubner's first book, "Freakonomics," is subtitled, "A Rogue Economist Explores The Hidden Side Of Everything." The opinion here is that what almost always turns out to be "hidden," is self-interest.

Four subcategories of altruistic behavior are patriotism, volunteerism, religious prosociality and environmentally responsible behavior (ERB). Patriotism is often seen as an altruistic act but can also be explained in terms of other less noble motivations. "Serving my country" can make *me* feel good in a number of ways. Having an identity as a soldier may earn respect within my family, my peers or society as a whole, not to mention increasing my own self-respect. It can provide me with a career, with security, with money for education, with status, with adventure, and can be an outlet for my competitive instincts. Or it can reduce my fear of not knowing what I want to do with my life, or a fear that I won't be able to earn a living, or of being a failure in school or in life in general. Plus everyone looks better in a uniform.

Evidence for this is found in the rather severe recession of 2008, for which there are more than enough volunteers for our armed services. Did the wars in Iraq and

---

[70] Levitt, S. & Dubner, S.J. op cit.

Afghanistan just become more fun? No, the services provide a home, a lifestyle, an opportunity and security all in one. I weigh my options, and if other roads look bleak, the army starts looking a lot better. Combined with clever marketing programs young people, who feel invincible anyway, line up to "serve their country."

Politicians, too, assert patriotism as the reason for throwing their hats in the ring, despite evidence to the contrary. "...politicians feel compelled to perform an elaborate pantomime of unalloyed altruism, asserting that self-interest and self-satisfaction are nowhere in the equation of their ambitions. They're doing it for us. They'd really rather not. The sacrifice is endurable, only because the cause is so important. Oh Please. ...I propose that candidates quit the pretense and lose the lofty language. No more talk about heeding "a call," whether it's from God, voters or Verizon."[71]

Volunteerism can be explained in a similar fashion. The volunteer gets the same thing out of his act that a donor does, starting with a "warm glow" of knowing you've helped someone. Consider the example of a father, John, who wants to coach his son or daughter's baseball/softball team. First, it gives John quality time with his child and gives them something to bond over. His child is likely to want John to be his coach, and it's tough to say "no" to your child. John's own Dad may have coached him so it brings up good memories for him. It might make John feel slightly important and civic minded, and give him a small amount of status among his peers. It also lets John recapture the days when he played ball and keeps him involved in sports, which he loves. It assures that his son/daughter will get playing time since consciously or not consciously, there is a bias to play your own child. It also allows John to mollify his wife, who has accused him of being a couch potato, and to contribute to the chore load of the household by

---

71 Bruni, Frank. "Humble Service With a Side of Swag." New York Times Op-Ed, August 20, 2011.

doing something he enjoys, as opposed to cooking or cleaning. All in all, a confluence of positive rewards for John.

In still other cases, volunteerism becomes part of how a person defines herself or may fulfill a personal need. One woman may do crossword puzzles, another becomes involved in politics, a third is a frequent volunteer. It's something that is enjoyed and helps define us. A childless adult might enjoy mentoring a teenager. A grandmother might enjoy reading to the blind or helping children to learn to read. A man who always wanted an athletic son might volunteer to coach a boys' team.

Religious prosociality is the idea that those who believe in God do good works for others more than non-religious people. Research doesn't lend much support, however. A review and analysis of the literature indicates that people, in effect, give more primarily when someone (or God) is watching or they think someone is watching.[72] That is, they are concerned about their reputation. The more someone cares about what people think of them, the more "altruistic" they will appear. Altruistic behavior, as found by Levitt and Dubner, is closely related to motives that make one feel better, such as reducing guilt, preserving ones reputation, or that carries some future expectation of having a favor returned.

Even on the level of foreign aid to underdeveloped countries, altruism is hard to find. The United Nations passed a resolution in 1970 stating that developed nations would set aside 0.7% of each of their Gross National Income to aid for poor countries. In fact, the amount actually dedicated has worked out to .25%, a little more than a third of what was mandated. This despite that around 80% of people surveyed in developed nations *say*

---

[72] Norenzayan, Ara & Shariff, Azim F. "The Origin and Evolution of Religious Prosociality," Science, Vol. 322, October 3, 2008, p. 58.

they are willing to pay more taxes to help poor people.[73] So while it is the socially acceptable thing to appear altruistic, when it gets down to brass tacks, self-interest seems to win out, even on a national level.

The idea that altruism can explain environmentally responsible behavior (ERB) has also been debunked. De Young invokes the term "intrinsic satisfaction" which subsumes feelings of competence, frugality and community participation as confluent contributors to ERB. Not by coincidence, intrinsic satisfaction is in large part similar to self-interest, as defined here. De Young adds that self-interest, ironically, which used to be seen as a source of environmental problems, may be part of the solution if financial incentives are available for ERB.[74] [75]

Hungerford & Volk[76] examined the effectiveness of environmental education in producing responsible behavior in the citizenry. Much of their analysis is based on a meta-study by Hines et. al.,[77] which looked at 128 different research projects. Major variables that were thought to contribute to ERB were sensitivity to the environment,

---

[73] Leiserowitz, Anthony A., Kates, Robert W. & Parris, Thomas M. "Sustainability Values, Attitudes, and Behaviors: A Review of Multinational and Global Trends. Annu. Rev. Environ. Resour. 2006. 31:413-44.

[74] De Young, Raymond. "Expanding and Evaluating Motives for Environmentally Responsible Behavior." Journal of Social Issues, Vol. 56, No. 3, 2000, pp. 509-526.

[75] See also: Kaplan, Stephen. "Human Nature and Environmentally Responsible Behavior." Journal of Social Issues, Vol. 56, No. 3, 2000, pp. 491-508.

[76] Hungerford, Harold R. & Volk, Trudi L. "Changing Learner Behavior Through Environmental Education." Journal of Environmental Education, 21(3), 1990, p.8-22.

[77] Hines, J.M., et. al. "Analysis and Synthesis of research on responsible environmental behavior: A meta-analysis." Journal of Environmental Education, 18(2), 1986/87, p. 1-8.

knowledge about the issues, personal investment, having the skills to act, feeling responsible to act and having the intention to act. Promoting ERB still has a long way to go, however, because the authors conclude, "when current reports on environmental quality are considered, we must admit that we have not been successful, on a widespread basis, in convincing world citizens to act in environmentally responsible ways."[78] The reason, I believe, for the lack of success is because self-interest has not been taken into account.

Let's consider some simple environmentally responsible behaviors, such as buying a "green" car, driving less miles, littering, recycling, and buying energy-saving light bulbs. Selfonomics would posit many possible self-interest-based reasons for ERB:

> 1) <u>Early Teaching</u>: We are taught not to litter and to recycle when we are young and thus these behaviors are in our comfort zones; they are part of how we define ourselves. Likewise, it makes us feel as if we are better parents if we serve as good environmental role models for our own children and feel that we are preparing them well to be good citizens. Thus we have learned to be proud of ourselves (DSI) or less guilty (PSI) if we recycle.

> 2) <u>Saving a Buck</u>: It makes financial sense for us, e.g. we save money, in the long run, on gas, or our car lasts longer if we drive less. Note that people who are less affluent (or poor) may not have the

---

[78] Hungerford & Volk, op. cit.

choice to drive anything but an old gas guzzler; the used clunker that more affluent people have traded in. And they probably have less control over having a flexible schedule to avoid traffic or the ability to telecommute. To the poor, being green is likely to be a luxury.

3) Vested Interest: If I live near the shore, I may feel ownership of local ecological issues, such as pollution of the ocean and beach erosion. Someone from the midwest would not have the same incentive.

4) Guilt Reduction: If I have a lot of money and a big house, one way I can feel less guilty about my success is to drive a hybrid.

5) Shame Avoidance: If I don't recycle, or drive a gas guzzler, I may face social ostracism, especially in circles of more educated people.

6) Self-Image Boost: I feel virtuous when I change the lighting in my house from the old wasteful incandescent bulbs to the new energy-saving fluorescents.

7) Avoidance of Penalties: By not littering and by recycling, I avoid potential fines.

There are some expressions of self-interest that work *against* ERB. Examples are:

1) <u>Absence of Ownership</u>: I am less likely to care about beach erosion if I live in Oklahoma than if I live in New Jersey.

2) <u>Ignorance</u>: I am not well-educated and don't know about environmental issues.

3) <u>Misinformation</u>: I am misinformed about science, as are many deniers of climate change.

4) <u>Spite</u>: I might want to "stick it to the man" by throwing my empty soda bottles or candy wrappers on the ground. I may feel disenfranchised in society and littering may represent a small act of rebellion.

5) <u>Poverty</u>: As mentioned above, if I am poor, I am likely to buy food and shelter in preference to a greener car. When one considers that ERB is a tough sell in an affluent country like the United States, attempting change globally will be daunting.

6) <u>Laziness</u>: Recycling requires extra effort, so I avoid it.

It is firmly believed that to be effective in inculcating ERB, environmental education must take into account all of the flavors of self-interest, whether they are Direct (saving money, boosting self-image), Protective (guilt reduction, avoidance of fines) or Misguided (spite, laziness).

In sum, all the attempts to pin down altruism seem to come to naught. There are altruistic, charitable and patriotic *acts*, as well as volunteerism and environmentally responsible *behavior*, but not altruism. Altruistic acts are not all that commonplace and selfless as they seem on the surface. Reading about the misery left in a hurricane's wake makes me realize how fortunate I am in relation to the victims, which invokes a good deal of guilt. One way to lessen the guilt is to give money. Plus donating to such a cause is generally felt as a virtuous act. So whether other people know I have given doesn't matter. I *feel* virtuous, which is good for me.

We all need or like to see ourselves as good, generous and helpful because it serves our self-interest. Thus it would not be surprising if people a) see themselves as "givers" whenever they do a nice thing for someone, b) remember things in a way that they were more giving than they were or gave more frequently than they actually did, for the same reason, and c) through selective memory remember doing something nice to "pay back" a friend, but forget it was payback. A useful term for doing just enough nice things for others so as to feel that we are good people (and selectively remembering them) is "token altruism."

Another slant on the same topic is that if other people know that I've given, then I feel virtuous in relation to them and, in a minor way, superior to them. It is also a good feeling for me to know that I've "put my money where my mouth is," after having discussed the slowness of the governmental response to a disaster with many of my friends. Do I feel bad for the people who were victims? Yes, of course. But my actions make *me* feel better.

An interesting, and perhaps extreme, interpretation of altruism comes from Bruce Bueno de Mesquita. He even throws Mother Teresa under the bus. "Could it be that Mother Teresa's ambition for herself was tied to her faith in an eternal reward? It makes sense to pay the price of sacrifice for the short finite time of a life span if the consequence is a reward that goes on for infinity in heaven. In fact, isn't that exactly the explanation many of us give for the actions of suicide bombers, dying in their own prideful eyes as martyrs who will be rewarded for all eternity in heaven?" [79] As Nicholas Thompson, reviewing the book for the New York Times notes, "Yes, you read that correctly. ...Bueno de Mesquita equates Mother Teresa with the likes of Mohamed Atta."[80]

An educated guess is that the number of altruistic acts that people perform varies from person to person and is normally distributed. People who enjoy volunteering or donating will be on one end of the curve and those that disdain it will be on the other, with the vast majority of people being in the middle. The amount of pleasure that people derive from their altruistic acts is also likely to be normally distributed, and both genetic and learned. Some get much pleasure from their altruistic acts so it serves their self-interest directly. Others get little intrinsic satisfaction from their altruistic acts and perform them only if someone is watching, if they want to save face, or if they want to score points with someone (e.g. political donations). The way to tell if the person really gets something out of giving is to keep it anonymous or hide the source of the donation.

What is clear is that waiting for altruistic action to solve problems will come to naught. We are driven by self-interest and any effective solutions, be they individual, local or global, will have to not only recognize this, but actually take advantage of it. Whether we're talking about climate change or international diplomacy, self-interest must be factored in to the discussion.

---

[79] Bueno de Mesquita, Bruno. (2009). *The Predictioneer's Game: Using the Logic of Brazen Self-Interest to See and Shape the Future.* Random House, New York.

[80] Thompson, Nicholas. New York Times Book Review, November 8, 2009.

CHAPTER 12: THE AMERICAN DREAM

According to a background article for children's studies at the Library of Congress,

> ...the American Dream has become the pursuit of material prosperity - that people work more hours to get bigger cars, fancier homes, the fruits of prosperity for their families - but have less time to enjoy their prosperity. Others say that the American Dream is beyond the grasp of the working poor who must work two jobs to insure their family's survival. Yet others look toward a new American Dream with less focus on financial gain and more emphasis on living a simple, fulfilling life.[81]

In looking for a definition, Matthew Warschauer comments that,

> One component of the American Dream seems, however, to be fairly consistent: the quest for money. Few will deny that Americans are intently focused on the "almighty dollar." In a society dedicated to capitalism and the maxim that, "the one who dies with the most toys wins," the ability to purchase a big house and a nice car separates those who are considered successful from those who are not. Yet the

---

[81] From a lesson plan for teachers available at the Library of Congress: http://lcweb2.loc.gov/learn/lessons/97/dream/thedream.html

question remains, how does one achieve this success? How is the Dream realized? For many Americans the formula is one of instant, albeit elusive, gratification. Rather than adhering to a traditional work ethic, far too many Americans are pinning their hopes on what they perceive as "easy" money.[82]

It's hard to envision pursuing the American Dream without invoking the concept of money, at least as an intermediary, if not as an end in itself. As the framers of the Constitution put it, "life, liberty, and the pursuit of happiness" comes with the territory if you are an American. Trying to make money through hard work or investment is not out of the ordinary. It is part of all of us, it is what we are taught, it is the way that the pursuit of self-interest is most obvious, and is most understandable to us. Perhaps those pesky framers misspoke. Perhaps it should have been "Me the People," not "We the People."

Take a 30 year old hard-working man named Bill, who earns eighteen dollars an hour at a major box store chain, such as Walmart in the year 2006. He has a wife and three young children, and they all live in a cramped two bedroom apartment. They pay $700 per month in rent, not including utilities. Bill has a high school education and doesn't see a way to increase the family earnings, aside from taking an occasional side job helping his friend do home repairs when the chance comes along.

Bill's boss, Tom, has a friend Ron, who just got a mortgage to buy a small house. Bill hears that Ron got what seems like a ridiculously low mortgage rate that sounds too good to be true. One day, over coffee, Bill hears it from Ron himself. Ron borrowed enough to buy a

---

[82] Warshauer, Matthew. "Who Wants To Be A Millionaire: Changing conceptions of the American Dream." American Studies Today Online, posted 2/13/2003. http://74.125.95.132/search?q=cache:29bkgeca2mgJ:www.americansc.org.uk/online/American_Dream.htm+%22american+dream%22&cd=3&hl=en&ct=clnk&gl=us&client=safari

small two bedroom home in a decent part of town that needs a lot of work. The mortgage was an "interest-only," no points, low-rate loan, with a "balloon" after three years. Ron explains that "balloon" means that the interest rate might jump from 3% to 9%, but because the price of houses seems to always go up, it will be easy to redo the loan with a fixed rate, or to get another low rate interest-only loan when the three years are up. Ron offers to hook Bill up with his mortgage broker, Sue.

Bill makes an appointment with Sue quickly, and can't believe what he hears from her. The payments on a house, similar to the one Ron bought, would only be $750 a month including real estate taxes. Since they will be able to deduct interest paid and real estate taxes on their Federal return, his family will end up paying less to own than to rent. Bill goes home and discusses it with his wife Katy, who's a little scared, but excited at the same time. They both like and trust Bill's boss, Tom, and feel he wouldn't have steered them wrong.

Within a few months, Bill, Katy and their kids are in their own place. Small, though bigger than the apartment they lived in, with a washer-dryer, a basement for the kids to play in, two bedrooms, a garage, and even a back yard. The place needs some work, but Bill is a good Mr. Fix-It, and things slowly get into shape. Bill and Katy have finally realized their American Dream...

...which lasts almost exactly three years, during which period the country goes into recession and the real estate market tanks. The hoped-for rise in home prices, which would allow for the remortgaging of a balloon loan, doesn't happen. When Bill and Katy talk to their bank, they are denied remortgaging, since house prices have declined and they have negative equity. Their mortgage payment goes from $762 to $1421 a month. Having no equity in the house, they have little incentive to keep making unaffordable payments, and walk away as the house falls into foreclosure.

Do we blame them for chasing the Dream? They are like all the rest of us. Trying to do the best they can for their family and themselves. Did they do anything wrong, or immoral, or illegal? Not at all. They played by the rules, followed their self-interest (which was not even misguided), had bad timing, and lost.

But what about Sue, the mortgage broker. At the time she was "helping" Bill and Katy get their home, one can easily imagine her sitting in a meeting with other brokers, and the regional manager telling them that they are on a mission to help people chase that American Dream. The more the merrier. The money is available to be lent, and it's their job to lend it. For Sue and her counterparts, the more they lend, the more money they themselves make, in the process of fulfilling their own American Dream. Again, nothing wrong, immoral or illegal. In fact, mortgage brokers in most states have no "fiduciary duty," i.e. the responsibility on the part of the broker to act in the best interest of their client. In other words, the borrower has to look out for themselves. Unfortunately, the ones who need to be the most careful are also the ones who are probably the most naive as to financial matters. Not that financial wizards could have predicted the precipitous drop in the housing market either.

What about Lucy, Sue's regional manager, or Craig, the CEO of the bank that's handing out the money? The same argument seems to apply. Each is trying to increase business to make more money for a) the company, which will reflect well on them, and b) themselves, so that they can chase their own American Dreams. As long as they are playing by the existing rules, which they are, what's the problem? Again, the problem is that the market for houses turned around, and no one saw it coming.

And how about Ernie and Cynthia in 2006? A couple in their fifties, they took $20,000 of equity out of their house in Ohio (which was nearly paid off) to buy a condominium in Florida. Actually, that's not quite accurate. They heard through friends in their suburban neighborhood that it was easy to "flip" a condominium in a resort area, because the prices were going up so fast. The idea was to get in at a "pre-construction price," by putting down their $20,000, wait six months to a year until the unit was built, and then sell the *right* to buy that unit at a higher price. They wouldn't even actually have to close on the condo. The unit they chose, was initially priced at $225,000 and, according to past results of close friends who bought in an earlier phase of the same development, they expected the unit to sell for at least $250,000 when that phase was completed. They figured that they'd gross a $25,000 profit and, after allowing $5,000 for expenses, net $20,000 on their initial investment. In effect, they'd double their money in less than a year. Since the couple was planning for retirement, every little bit of money they could accumulate was important.

While reading a few articles on the supposed "greed" involved in flipping a condo, Ernie and Cynthia were upset by the accusation of avarice. They were doing nothing illegal, in fact someone was going to make money from the condominium that they bought. Why shouldn't it be them? Over the last year, as their friends reported their success stories, Ernie and Cynthia felt left out. They worked hard to accumulate equity in their house. Why not put it to work for their retirement?

The same brick wall that Bill and Katy encountered was the same one that Ernie and Cynthia ran into. When the housing market turned around, the prices of houses in general started to fall. Those in resort areas, such as Florida, were overbuilt and fell even faster. A condominium identical to the one that Ernie and Cynthia put their deposit down on when it was priced at $225,000, was now selling for $175,000. Even at that price, the units weren't selling. There were simply no buyers. Now the couple had two choices; either close on their condo, coming up with another $205,000 to make the contract price, knowing that even if they did, the unit wasn't worth it, or walk away. The decision was a no-brainer. Their best and only choice was to forfeit their hard earned $20,000. And again, no one saw it coming.

Actually, it wouldn't have mattered if someone did see it coming. One would need not only prescience, but enormous self-confidence and a whole lot of guts. How do you forecast gloom and doom when everyone around you, including your boss, your reports, and even you, are making money hand over fist? What would be the reaction of those around you if you said, "We need to stop doing what we are doing?"

Consider the related situation of working within the brokerage industry. You are Ken, the successful stockbroker. How do you stand up, when the Dow is around 14,000,[83] and say, "I think this is going to end soon and we'd better run for the hills?" As a stockbroker, you make money when people are buying stocks or selling them to buy others, and also make a few bucks on the side trading for your own account. Your bosses are happy because commissions are flowing in the door, your customers are happy as they watch the value of their retirement accounts increase, and even your wife is happy with her wonderful husband Ken, because this year's bonus was bigger than the one given last year. Felipe, Ken's boss's boss's boss, is especially happy. Because of his experience and track record, he has a million dollar guaranteed bonus built into his contract which is not based on the performance of the company. Apparently executives like Felipe are in short supply and it behooves the company to pay dearly to make sure that he doesn't leave to work for the competition. Felipe, being the loyal employee that he is, is happy to oblige them.

Again, as with those involved with mortgages, there is no illegality here, no immorality. Sure, you're making more money than you ever dreamed you'd earn, but you're

---

[83] In October, 2007, the Dow Jones Industrial Index was a little over 14,000. Seventeen months later, in March, 2009, it had dropped to around 6,500!

providing an important service in our capitalistic society, and you work long hours and have tons of stress that people outside the industry could never understand. You are responsible for people's life savings. Their self-interest is confluent with your own. You deserve the money you are paid. Also, you're not getting any younger and have to make hay while the sun shines.

How, under these conditions, do you say "no mas?" You don't. You look around and everyone you work with, including your boss, seems to have confidence that the gravy train will continue. The most you might do is make some minor comments to your customers, saying, "You might want to cover yourself on the downside by...," but you won't push it for fear of looking like a doomsayer or a chicken. The "experts" see no problem with what's going on, saying that the worst that will happen is that the market may plateau or move "sideways" for awhile (stay level). You're afraid of the ridicule and damage to your reputation that will occur if you stand up and blow the whistle which you are not even sure should be blown. You don't have enough confidence in your naysaying to stick your neck out like that. Plus you're still making lots of money. Until you're not, because the market has tanked.

Okay, let's figure out whose fault this is. Were Bill, Katy, Ernie, Cynthia, Ken and Felipe all just greedy? Was it their overarching desire to make money or get rich the cause of the crash? Should they blame themselves, or should we blame them? Are they just pursuing their self-interest, or are they greedy?

An online dictionary defines greed as "excessive or rapacious desire, especially for wealth or possessions." It is certainly not complimentary to be called "greedy." But what is excessive? Who defines what is too much? Are Bill Gates and Warren Buffett greedy? They certainly have more than they need. How about the couple with one child living in a $1,000,000, 5,000 square foot home? They don't need all that space. How about the woman with the four karat diamond or big Mercedes, or the guy with the 40 foot fishing boat, the $10,000 Rolex or $3,000 golf clubs? It may turn out that greed is attributed to people that have more than us, especially those people that we don't like or don't get along with or don't know.

The founders of our country intended us to "pursue happiness." Nowhere did they specify how much happiness is "happiness." We live in a capitalistic society, which encourages competition, acquisition and self-interest. What's the problem? It may turn out that those that we call "greedy people" are little more than those who are the most successful, through talent or luck, at pursuing their ISI. If we could measure the quality and quantity of each person's self-interest on a numerical scale, the amount of direct self-interest is likely to be normally distributed. Those with the highest amount of self-interest would likely be seen as aggressive, selfish, covetous and thus greedy, especially if they are successful. But is greed, seen this way, bad?

Schumpeter talks about "creative destruction," in which free market economies end up replacing old methods and products with new ones.[84] Due to competition, and the rewards of being successful, free markets encourage entrepreneurs, people willing to take risks to develop new business models, products and processes. The fruits of the work of the entrepreneur replace old products and processes and with new ones. Hence "creative destruction," in that as new ideas create, their use destroys, old ways of doing things. Seen this way, entrepreneurship is built into capitalism and free market economies. Are entrepreneurs, who basically want to play "top of the hill" and win, greedy? So not only are our political roots, thanks to our Founding Fathers, encouraging greed, but so are the economic underpinnings of our capitalist society.

Maybe the problem is with our system, which may be the best history has to offer, but is not perfect. Most of

---

[84] Schumpeter, Joseph. (1942). Capitalism, Socialism and Democracy.

the problems we've encountered stem from legal, not illegal, acts. When you take normal human self-interest and add competition within a capitalist society, which is sanctioned and actually encouraged by the rule book that is our Constitution, you end up with people trying to get ahead, all playing by the rules. (Note that we're not talking about people who skirt the law to make money illegally.)

The problem seems to be with the rules by which we have to play. If Bill and Katy can borrow money for a house without having money down, and able to pay on an interest-only loan, we may be asking for trouble. If mortgage companies are not required to vet applicants carefully, we may be in for trouble. If Ernie and Cynthia are allowed to put a small percentage of the price of a second home and have no obligation to close on that home, problems may ensue. If Ken the stockbroker and Felipe, his superior, are entrenched in a system that discourages or punishes contrarian thinking, no one will favor caution. And if participants can take huge risks with other people's money, make millions if they win, but lose little or nothing if their bets don't pan out, we're asking for trouble. In all three cases, the rules allow behavior that come with unintentional consequences that come into play when the economy hits a wall.

Without getting too detailed, the Bush administration favored a hands-off approach to the markets. The Security and Exchange Commission, headed by Christopher Cox, let the markets relatively unfettered. Cox, who resigned when Barack Obama took office, was thought to have been lax in overseeing the financial industry, and being blind to the woes of the banking industry and to the machinations of hedge funds.

One infamous example of how the lack of careful oversight led to catastrophe, which can be blamed on no one person in particular, was the phenomenon of "credit default swaps" (CDSs). If I own a position in a Company X, I generally make money as long as that company does. But what if I'm the nervous type, who is pretty sure that

Company X will thrive, but am worried about the economy in general, or the industry that Company X competes in? I want to be sure, if Company X takes a nosedive, that I don't lose everything. So I look to insure my investment. I buy a "policy" through which I pay a small premium, say one percent of the value of my position per year to a second party, who guarantees that if Company X goes belly up, I get all my money back. I'm willing to pay one percent a year since for the last few years I've made eight percent on my investment. I figure that a guaranteed seven percent is even better. So far so good.

The problem comes in though, because I can buy this same insurance on Company Y, which I don't own. I do this if I think there's a chance that the market as a whole may be headed downward, or I think that Company Y in particular may be in trouble. Further, any Harry, Gary, Barry and Larry can do the same as I did, namely buying default insurance on Company Y without owning it. And, unfortunately, the guy who sold me and the guys this insurance on Company Y is *not* required to have enough reserves to pay off people buying this insurance. In 2008, the demise of Lehman Brothers and the sale of Bear Stearns were indirect results of this system. In effect, once there was a hint of financial difficulty, people started buying downside insurance on Bear Stearns. This, in turn, led to people losing confidence in the company and selling the stock, the inability of Bear to borrow money, and more selling of stock. No one seemed to know that this was a problem until after the dam gave way.

Another, concurrent problem occurred with the bundling of mortgages. If say, 5,000 people take out mortgages, these mortgages can be resold to a separate entity which puts together, or "bundles," these mortgages in one big lump. The lump is then "securitized," i.e., broken into shares, and the shares sold on the market. A person or institution can buy a stake in this security, having the expectation of say, a 5% return, based on the aggregated monthly mortgage payments from the original 5,000 people. Again, so far so good.

What happens, though, when an unusual number of these mortgages are not paid and end up in foreclosure? That's what happened when, and as, the real estate market crashed. The 5% return that was anticipated evaporates, and the value of the securitized "lump" sinks rapidly. Further, because these lumps are aggregated, it's difficult to know how many of the mortgages are in trouble. Many of the biggest banks got stuck with these securitized lumps, which were worth much less than they paid for them, and of undefined value. So the banks went the way of the Wall Street firms. Down.

We began discussing the American Dream by referring to ordinary people looking out for their self-interest and that of their loved ones, and ended up with financial crises. The issue seems not to be self-interest in itself, because that is inevitable, but the quality of the rules and laws that *channel* that self-interest. We are simple creatures who, when confronted by very complex financial situations, find it easier to keep our heads in the sand. The less transparent the rules and systems are, the less we are aware, and the more opportunity there is for trouble.

Let's see what all of these attempts to grab the American Dream have in common:

1) They all start with (primarily) direct individual self-interest with one person (and perhaps his or her family by extension) trying to make money and/or make their lives better.

2) This DSI leads them to seek out situations which will allow them to make more money or improve their lifestyle. These include buying a home, or a second home, trying to make money at real estate by flipping a condo, or selling a mortgage, or trying to sell stocks to make commissions, or to bundle mortgages and make a "cut" of the action, or to

prevent losing money by hedging bets on a credit default swaps.

3) These opportunities are not available to all citizens. For many of us, the only way to better ourselves financially is to work longer hours, take a second job, or look for a new job that pays more money per hour. Hard work is the basis of the Protestant work ethic,[85] and is almost universally seen as laudable. Other routes to wealth are often seen, especially by the have-nots, as greed.

4) No one believes that what they are doing is a product of greed. All have reasons or rationalizations for what they do, some of which are:

    a) It's the American Dream. That's what we're all supposed to do in America.

    b) Everyone else makes money by investing in houses or stocks, so why shouldn't I?

    c) I work hard and deserve to be rewarded for my efforts.

    d) It's not illegal, so why shouldn't I do it?

    e) I need to grab the opportunity when it presents itself.

    f) I'm only doing it for my family, so my kids can go to college.

----

[85] Weber, Max. (2002) The Protestant Ethic and The Spirit of Capitalism. Penguin Books; translated by Peter Baehr and Gordon C. Wells.

g) I'm not hurting anyone else by doing what
   I do (selling mortgages, making
   commissions on stock sales).

Note that we've always presupposed that a person supporting their SI does so within the law. If we assume that DSI is distributed on the normal curve, then aggressive seeking of self-interest will be high on one end. It would not be surprising if some of these aggressive people "cross the line," that is, take illegal routes to sating their self-interest. Taking minor situations, such as speeding while driving, or cheating on your tax return may be illustrative.

Steve is usually in a hurry. He's a type-A personality, and drives 75 m.p.h in a 65 m.p.h. zone, whenever he can. He will tailgate, and silently curses those who choose to obey the speed laws. How does he rationalize that behavior? Steve thinks he's a better driver than most (cockiness) and will tell you that everyone does it. That he's just keeping up with traffic. He doesn't plan to speed, but when he gets into the "game," he finds he's back driving at 75. Once he becomes a speeder, it's hard to then go back to doing the speed limit. He also knows that it is unlikely that he will be stopped because police usually have a 10 mile per hour latitude, an unofficial law, so that 65 really means 75.

Similar arguments might be made for Jimmy, who takes liberties with his tax returns. Jimmy earns $50,000 at his day job and around $7,000 a year doing odd jobs around the apartment complex in which he and his family live. The day job gives him a W-2 at the end of the year, and all of this money is reported to the IRS. Payments for the odd jobs come in dribs and drabs and are almost always in cash. Somehow, this money goes right into Jimmy's pocket and never makes it to his tax return forms. Jimmy's reasons include everyone else is doing it, he and his family deserve that money, he's always done it, and he couldn't live without that money now, and it's not hurting anyone. He also knows, from experience, that the IRS probably won't bother him because he is "small fish"; in effect there is an unofficial rule that certain people aren't worth pursuing.

If you compare the reasons of Steve the Speeder and Jimmy the Handy Man to that of the average person that *does not* break the law, you will not see a huge difference between or among them. Using a law enforcement concept, "means, motive, opportunity," might explain the difference between those that stay within the law, and those who step over the line (other things, such as how people are raised, being equal). For Jimmy, he has the means (he's handy), the motive (self-interest) and opportunity (he lives in a place where people need his services). If Jimmy was not handy (no means), had less of a motive (his wife worked and he wasn't so in need of extra money), or he lived in an area flooded with handy-persons, he may not have ended up breaking the law.

The rationales of those that abide the law and those that break it are not much different. If anything, they are differences of degree and not kind.   All of the people named in this chapter are looking out for themselves, think it's normal, and think that everyone else is doing the same thing.   They are all chasing the American Dream, as laid out for us by our forefathers and, for the most part are doing it within the customs, rules or laws that society lays down. Although we can allege that the problem lies with greedy people, the so-called "greed" is self-interest by degrees that is integral to human nature. The problem lies with the customs, rules and laws within which that self-interest is allowed to operate.

PART IV: FROM "WE THE PEOPLE" TO "ME THE PEOPLE"

It is not too much of a stretch to say that self-interest drastically influences life in our country and, in fact, the world as we know it. The financial crisis was brought on by millionaires aspiring to be billionaires. Our political system can be at least partially bought by wealthy people or corporations (who/which the Supreme Court equated to individuals) that dump tons of money into targeted races to defeat vulnerable opponents, in effect buying Congressional seats.[86] [87] The internet allows one person to reach many and have an inordinate influence on the masses. Religion, which is intended to bring hope and solace to humanity, often sows rifts and breeds hostility.

---

[86] For example, "The anonymously financed conservative groups that have played such a crucial role this campaign year are starting a carefully coordinated final push to deliver control of Congress to Republicans, shifting money among some 80 House races they are monitoring day by day. ...Officials involved in the effort over the midterm elections' final week say it is being spearheaded by a core subset of the largest outside conservative groups, which have millions of dollars left to spend on television advertisements, mailings and phone calls for five potentially decisive Senate races, as well as the scores of House races. From Rutenberg, Jim. "Pro-Republican Groups Prepare Big Push at End of Races." New York Times, October 24, 2010, p.1.

[87] Speaking of the financial sector, Frank Rich notes, "Now corporations of all kinds can buy more of Washington than before, thanks to the Supreme Court's Citizens United decision and the rise of outside "nonprofit groups" that can legally front for those who prefer to donate anonymously." Rich, Frank. "Still the Best Congress Money Can Buy." New York Times, November 27, 2010.

Add the fallibility of humans and what emerges is a recipe for disaster. We can only process a certain amount of information. None of us has time to digest the myriad of data flung at us or available to us on a daily basis. So we latch on to something that seems to make sense and we don't dig much deeper,[88] leaving us open to bias and truthiness.[89] We are also competitive by nature (self-interest honed by evolution), and have a need to root for something, be it a baseball team, a political candidate or a religion. This leads to a corollary of truthiness, namely "proofiness," wherein we bend numbers to prove our point.[90] We also have a need to be popular, so choices (political candidates, sides of issues, music, cars) may be at least partially based, consciously or not, on what gives us currency in our social circle. For some, making an unpopular choice makes us feel better about ourselves and helps our self-image. And things happen so much faster today than in the past, leaving us little time to react to one event before the next occurs.

It may be that the best we can do is at least know that we are stupid by degrees; that is, recognize that we can't take in everything and are all susceptible to bias so that, as Socrates said, "we know what we don't know." Examining the nature of the problems generated by self-interest may help us devise solutions.

---

[88] Disclosure: For this author, the leading source of input is the New York Times (both online and print). I don't have time to read everything, so I trust the Times for approximately 40% of my input, the rest being from television news (20%), Time & Newsweek magazines (15%) and National Public Radio (10%) and social science periodicals (10%). The remainder comes to me in my sleep.

[89] op. cit.

[90] op. cit.

CHAPTER 13: GREED

Stories of lust make us sit up and take notice. We watch intently as one after another famous person damages or throws away their private life and career for some forbidden fruit. Governors Mark Sanford, Jim McGrevey and Elliot Spitzer, presidential candidates Gary Hart and John Edwards, President Bill Clinton, IMF head Dominique Strauss-Kahn and, of course, the once squeaky-clean sports idol Tiger Woods We marvel at what we assume is their lack of judgment, yet because they themselves and their family are the main victims, we do feel a bit of sympathy for them.

Greed, another of the Seven Deadly Sins, is a little less sensational, and receives little sympathy from the masses, perhaps because it is seen as premeditated as opposed to a result of passion, and because the victims are other than the perpetrator(s). Since the families of the greedy people benefit, there is little compassion for them either.

Lust is more black and white. You either cheat on your spouse or you don't (although the issue of internet pornography is a gray area). Greed is by degrees, which presents a problem: who is greedy and who is not? Where is the cutoff point? For example, in 2010, the corporate tax rate for General Electric was 7.4% because the company took full *legal* advantage of all tax breaks available to it.[91] G.E. makes a good profit, keeps almost all of it, pays out generous dividends to its shareholders and takes care of its executives with pay and bonuses. Is this greed?

---

[91] Nocera, Joe. "Who Could Blame G.E.?" New York Times, Op-Ed, April 4, 2011.

OBVIOUS GREED

When times are good, excessive greed sails beneath our radar. But when a recession hits, as it did in 2008, the greedy make good headlines, and we sit up and take notice. For years, Wall Street bigwigs rode the crest of a decade-long wave of prosperity and were able to accumulate fortunes. Yet when the businesses they ran faltered, and their financial decisions negatively affected shareholders and John Q. Public, they still collected immodest year-end bonuses. We still tolerate their excesses. "This year [2010] alone, while millions of others suffer from the Great Recession, bankers and traders are expected to be paid - incredibly - another estimated $144 billion in compensation and benefits. Accordingly, Wall Street remains the No. 1 destination for our best and brightest."[92]

Once in a while, this angers us, Mr. and Mrs. Public. It seems, to us less fortunate ones, that they were being rewarded for failure. They were and are drinking top-shelf wine even as the holders of the company's stock and out-of-work employees are crying in their bottom-shelf beer.

Distribution of wealth in the United States provides a subtle example of the power of self-interest. How is it that although the overall wealth of the planet is growing, there are still so many people living in poverty? To answer the question, we can look at the Gross Domestic Product, or G.D.P. G.D.P. (for the U.S.) is the sum total of every bit of economic activity in the United States over a given period of time. Currently it's around 14 trillion dollars per year. "...the G.D.P. accurately calculates the dollar value that is created, for example, when workers put together steel, wires, rubber and upholstery to make an automobile. The car's value, which is the profit as well as the sum of the labor and parts, is incorporated into the total. The Federal Bureau of Economic Analysis adds them up four times a

---

[92] Cohan, William D. "The Power of Failure." New York Times, Opinionator, November 26, 2010.

year and announces whether the G.D.P. has risen...or fallen..."[93]

So what happens to the money that is made from those manufactured automobiles? Who benefits? Does it go to the people who made the car in the form of increased wages, does it go to stockholders, or does it go to executives, in the form of bonuses or stock options? Unfortunately, it seems that corporate executives have been the primary beneficiary of the bull market economy that ended in 2007. "...over the last 15 years...while the G.D.P. has continued to rise, wages have stagnated, pensions have shrunk or disappeared and *income inequality has increased* [italics ours].[94] [95] In effect, the wealthy are getting wealthier, while the less fortunate are having more trouble making ends meet. The reason for this "effect" can be traced to the people making the decisions, namely corporate executives putting their own needs first.

The playing field is anything but level. Charles Blow[96] refers to a 2011 Consumer Reports Employment Index which finds that over the last two years people with low incomes have lost more jobs than they have gained, while the more affluent classes have gained more jobs than they have lost. Those that have more are in a better position to acquire more.

[93] Uchitelle, Louis. "G.D.P. ≠ Happiness: Hey, Big Number, Make Room for the Rest of Us," New York Times Week in Review, 8/31/2008, p. 3.

[94] ibid.

[95] Also, Kroll, Andy. "The New American Oligarchy." Truthout, December 2, 2010.

[96] Blow, Charles. "Them That's Not Shall Lose." New York Times, Op-Ed, June 24, 2011.

LESS OBVIOUS GREED

But wait a minute. Should we only pick on the wealthy? Is it only they that want more? How about those Grandmas out there that fall for get rich quick schemes and lose all their hard earned savings to hustling con men. This time we all feel bad when they get taken to the cleaners, but doesn't it indicate greed also? The major difference is that this is greed exhibited by innocent people who have no concept of what they're getting themselves into. Sympathy can't make up for the disaster predicted by that combination of greed, ignorance and gullibility. It is tough, however, to think of less affluent people that risk money and lose it as greedy; while rich people bear no such burden.

Looking elsewhere, what about the average guy with a house and a pension fund who chooses risky options for allocating those funds and ends up losing his shirt when the market falls off a cliff? Or the woman who takes a big hit to her pension plan and panics, so that she sells at the bottom of the market, and then watches her stocks recover *after* they have been sold. It's sort of like kicking *yourself* when you're down. How about all of those ordinary people who jumped on the high-tech bandwagon in the late 1990s, only to lose everything when the bubble burst in the early 2000s? The ones who got in early and then turned cautious made out just fine. The ones who arrived late and stupid lost their shirts.

How about the silent majority, the great American middle class? Isn't it greedy to change jobs to make a few more dollars in your paycheck each week? In a good economy, this is seen as a legitimate and advisable way to "get ahead." In a bad market these job-hoppers could be last-in-first-out and regret jumping ship. Or the people who buy lottery tickets every day, spending thousands of dollars they can ill afford over the years, with the hope of hitting the jackpot? Are they just being greedy? It seems like it's not just the rich that want more money. Most of us are willing to take risks, some more than others, to make a buck. It seems that we are all built in very similar ways.

But, "Hold on!" you say indignantly. "I'm not greedy! Not me." We certainly never see *ourselves* as greedy. The other guy, maybe, but not me. But what if we're wrong? What if we're all greedy, by degrees? Maybe using the word "greed" isn't the best way to describe the behavior we're talking about. Greed seems to apply only to acquiring money or the things money can buy and describes most easily people who are particularly successful at accumulating wealth, not the ones that fail in the attempt. Is there a better term to use?

LESSONS FROM THE COUCH

I'm going to change subjects for a moment. I've been a psychotherapist for quite a while. I've noticed that almost everyone I see in counseling has a difficult time understanding the behavior of people that they deal with in life, be it at home or at work. Why does their significant other disagree with them so often? Why does their spouse want a divorce when they thought the marriage was going well? Why doesn't their teenager understand the importance of doing their homework?

As a therapist, I try to put myself in the position of the person they can't figure out. I try to "think as" the other by looking for that person's motivation. What drives him or her? What could have led them to act the way they did? Sometimes I use the conclusions I reach to better understand the whole situation, sometimes I feed back what I figured out to my patient, and sometimes I "play" the part of the other, for example the husband or wife that wanted out of the marriage and let the grieving spouse ask me questions.   Over the years, I've been told many times that, as far as the patient can tell, I'm usually pretty accurate. They recognize many of the phrases that I tick off to them, such as "You never listen to me," or "You always seem angry," or "I've been telling you that I'm unhappy for years but it went right over your head," as ones that they've heard from their significant other.

What am I actually doing? Yes, I've been around for a while and have seen many patients and situations, I'm more objective than they are, and can generalize well. But introspection tells me it's simply, if that word applies, figuring out what's "in it for them," "them" being the person I'm trying to figure out. I've always assumed that they are looking out for their own self-interest. And lo and behold, taking that perspective seems to work. The patient, his or her significant other, his or her kids, are all driven by their own, differing, self-interests.

IS GREED JUST A FLAVOR OF SELF-INTEREST?

How is this discussion related to greed, the subject with which we started? Well, it seems as though greed is little more than the most obvious and easily talked-about kind of self-interest. Or, self-interest is most apparent when it involves the acquisition of money. This conclusion is not exactly novel, as Adam Smith, the 18th century British philosopher posited self-interest as the basis for all economic markets several hundred years ago. But it's not just in economic matters that self-interest seems to be pervasive.

People also look out for their own interests in personal relationships. The spouse who wants out of a marriage and the teenager who goofs off when it comes to school are both looking out for themselves. As is the spouse who wants to spend every Sunday on the golf course, or every evening glued to the television, or the phone or the computer. Their choices may be partially or totally misguided and self-defeating, but nonetheless, we have normal everyday people looking out for number one.

Or consider the profession of being a salesperson. If I'm trying to sell you a widget, the only way you'll buy it is if *you* think that it is in your self-interest to do so (you need it, it has value, it will make you look/feel good, etc.). So as a salesperson, it is in *my* self-interest to convince you that

158

you need or want my widget. That's how I make my commission. In effect, I'm trying to convince you that buying the widget is in *your* self-interest because it is in *my* self-interest. To me, my self-interest comes first while yours is really known only to you and is almost irrelevant to me.

Is there a difference between people following their self-interest and greed? Although it is a little unsettling to equate the Grandma who falls for a phony investment scheme with a millionaire Wall Street executive, a car/insurance salesperson, a condominium flipper or an unscrupulous mortgage broker, the answer seems to be "no." Using some concepts that were discussed at length earlier in the book, here are some of the assumed similarities and differences:

1) It is assumed that everyone looks out for themselves, but by degrees. Most likely, observed Direct Self-Interest can fit a normal curve model, with some people possessing inordinately aggressive pursuit of self-interest (the greedy Wall Streeters), and others being timid in that regard (the Grandmas).

2) Some people look out for themselves by *protecting* themselves, i.e. avoiding pain rather than seeking pleasure. They buy lots of insurance, drive slowly, don't invest in high-flyers. They are "average Joes" that play the game of life cautiously. They are not likely to be seen as greedy, although they regularly follow their self-interest and keep themselves safe. PSI is also likely to be normally distributed.

3) Humans are eminently great rationalizers. A successful and well-paid baseball player, entertainer or businessperson will come to believe that he or she deserves the riches or accolades through hard work or talent. They will not think of themselves as greedy; rather justly rewarded. Anyway, a salary of twelve million a year doesn't go as far as most people think (we've heard).

4) Some people are just extremely good at what they do, be it as an entertainer, an athlete, a doctor/lawyer or a financial guru. Athletes strive to get better, entertainers improve their acts, and financial whizzes get better at making money. Talented people are sought out and can "charge" more for their services and people who are good at making more money are often called greedy. This is where the "means, motive and opportunity" argument comes in. Naive people who follow their self-interest but have little expertise are likely to lose money, and thus miss their chance to be thought of as "greedy."

5) People who break the law in attempts to make money, may be exhibiting self-interest, or may be seen as greedy, but they may also be crooks. Some people stretch the envelope and others go past even a semblance of honesty.

All in all, "greed" seems to be a word that applies to the **aggressive pursuit of monetary self-interest by people who are in the right place at the right time, and are successful at it.** They pursue fortune within the existing laws, and they rationalize their success by believing they deserve what they earn.

THE TAKEAWAY

It is not happenstance that self-interest pops up among all people when it comes to making money. Self-interest also appears in everyday life in our marriages, our families, our friendships, our jobs, our politics and our decisions and disagreements. In fact, it is averred that **humans act on self-interest *all* of the time, in *every* arena**.

CHAPTER 14: POLITICAL SELF-INTEREST

Examining political self-interest makes economic self-interest look like child's play. When it comes to economics, the choices are black and white, i.e. if a certain choice makes you more money, go for it. We all prefer to make more money to making less money. We all prefer that the prices of our houses and stocks go up rather than down.

Political choices, however, are less clear. Most choices in the political arena aren't right or wrong. They are just different, and matters of opinion. Are we for a strong national defense or not? Are we for or against stem cell research? Are we for or against cap-and-trade? Or free-trade agreements? Absolute right answers are much harder to come by in the political arena.

Economic values can be quantified and scaled. Political values are almost always matters of opinion, and therefore are not scaleable and aren't right or wrong. The 2008 Presidential election between McCain and Obama offered stark contrasts in values between the two sides. Obama won handily, 53% to 47%, yet almost half of the voting population thought their self-interest would be better served by a vastly different approach than the one offered by Obama. There is no right or wrong.

Anybody remember the phrase "It's the economy, stupid?," that arose in Bill Clinton's successful Presidential bid against George H. W. Bush in 1992. Bush was ahead, based on foreign policy successes toward the end of his term, but the economy went into recession during the 1992 campaign, and economic factors played a much larger role in peoples' decisions when they entered the voting booth. The implication of the phrase is that people vote for candidates based on how they think their pocketbooks will be affected. If I think that a candidate will leave me in better economic straits, they've got my vote, especially in hard times. If I think that candidate will leave me worse off financially, I'm voting for the other guy.

The interrelationship of self-interest, politics and economics is a complex one. The politics of self-interest seems to subsume the economics of self-interest. That is, while most economic issues eventually become political ones, not all political issues become economic ones (e.g. stem cell research, abortion, prejudice/hate crimes), although eventually, all political issues will have some economic consequences (e.g., states rights, Supreme Court nominations) down the road. Just as with economic issues however, all political ones involve voting one's self-interest.

We are under a sociocultural dictum to do so. The concept of our democratic nation, as proposed by the likes of Thomas Jefferson, Ben Franklin and their buddies, is that everyone is *supposed* to vote their self-interest. Lincoln's "of the people, by the people, for the people," (from the Gettysburg address) implies that every citizen's vote counts. Nowhere is it actually *written* that we should vote our self-interest, but it is *implied* over and over. Our Founding Fathers told us, in effect, to "look out for number one."

We also have a representative government, in which men and women are elected to represent our collective self-interest in the Senate and House of Representatives. If those representatives don't look out for our needs, don't get projects funded, he or she may not be reelected. In fact, our country is lousy with the legalized pursuit of self-interest, either directly by our votes, or indirectly through the people we elect. And occasionally, it is fraught with the illegal pursuit of self-interest, as in the saga of (now ex-) Governor Rod Blagojevich of Illinois and the late President Richard Nixon.

Then there is the "Citizens United" ruling by the Supreme Court of January, 2010, which allowed corporations to be treated as individuals when it comes to campaign donations. In effect, this ruling catalyzed but did not initiate, the takeover of the American political system by the wealthy. It also presents an interesting interplay between economic and political self-interests. "Before Citizens United, the rich used their wealth to subtly shape policy, woo politicians and influence elections. Now, with so much money flowing into their hands and the contribution faucets wide open, they can simply buy American politics so long as the price is right."[97]

One of many examples from the 2010 midterm elections is illustrative, though this story fortunately has a just ending. Bruce Braley, a Democrat from Iowa was targeted by Republicans wielding huge amounts of money and distorted messages. The American Future Fund spent over $500,000 and the U.S. Chamber of Congress roughly $250,000 attacking him by putting words in his mouth that he never uttered.[98] Neither of these organizations discloses its contributors. This particular election was not bought (Braley won reelection), but others were in 2010. This can be directly traceable to the Citizens United decision.

"The anonymously financed conservative groups that have played such a crucial role this campaign year are starting a carefully coordinated final push to deliver control of Congress to Republicans, shifting money among some 80 House races they are monitoring day by day."[99] The attempt to buy races is only thinly veiled. "'We carpet-bombed for two months in 82 races, now it's sniper time,' said Rob Collins, president of American Action Network,

[97] Kroll, Andy. "The New American Oligarchy." Truthout, December 2, 2010.

[98] "Secret Money in Iowa." New York Times Editorial, October 26, 2010.

[99] Rutenberg, Jim. "Pro-Republican Groups Prepare Big Push at End of Races." New York Times, October 25, 2010, p. A1.

which is one of the leading Republican groups this campaign season..."[100]

Another ingenious tactic used by Republicans is reported in an article in the New Yorker by Jane Mayer.[101] In 2010, Republican strategist Ed Gillespie ran a campaign called "REDMAP," at attempt to win back state legislatures in key states. In North Carolina, several hundred thousand dollars per contest were used to buy attack ads in small local races to unseat Democrats. Eighteen of 22 Democrats were replaced statewide, resulting in Republican majorities in both chambers of of the state legislature. One donor, Art Pope, gave over two million dollars to that effort, a game changing amount of money in small races. The Republican-controlled legislature is attempting to redistrict the state to increase partisan advantage in future races, including the 2012 Presidential election. Mayer's article points to outrageous innuendoes and untruths used in the attack ads. When this type of message is viewed by low-information voters who will not do any fact checking, the results are predictable: elections can be successfully bought. And Republicans haven't cornered this technique. Democrats aren't far behind.

Our forefathers, fought the tyranny and oppression of the British Crown vigorously, so that they could live and be free in a democratic system where each man had a vote. It's hard to believe that they would have been supportive of Citizens United and its April, 2014 follow-on, which gives inordinate power to those with money and one-sided agendas. It makes one wonder about and question the inviolability with which the Constitution is viewed.

---

[100] ibid

[101] Mayer, Jane. "State for Sale." The New Yorker, October 10, 2011.

Civility and collegiality is hard to find in the political arena.[102][103] Self-interest is so rampant that it has erased the existence of the dignified statesman, athlete or public figure. Sensationalism and schadenfreude has taken over our media. "The old dignity code has not survived modern life. The costs of its demise are there for all to see. Every week there are new scandals featuring people who simply do not know how to act."[104] So one lustful Senator replaces an avaricious business leader, replaces a steroid-enhanced athlete on the front page. And the self-interest of those reporting the news is slanted toward sensationalism because it sells, serving the self-interest of both the reporter and the news corporation. That is why it is vital that each of us become acutely aware of the source of any information we intend to ingest.

Part of the complexity of self-interest in the political arena is the array of issues that contribute to each voter's choice. I may have beliefs about foreign policy, domestic policy, right to life issues, immigration, Supreme Court nominations which have to be placed on a mental balance scale. Yet all of these have to be distilled down to a vote for (usually) one of two candidates.

It's not always clear cut. Take Warren as an example. In the upcoming Presidential election, he agrees with the views of both candidates, depending upon the issue. He's bombarded with advertisements and has no idea if they are truthful or not. He often falls back on the thinking that "they're all full of it." He belongs to a union, and the union favors Candidate A, but his girlfriend is a rabid fan of Candidate B and beats Warren over the head with her views. Who does he pull the lever for? It might

---

[102] Nocera, Joe. "The Last Moderate." New York Times Op-Ed, September 5, 2011.

[103] Lofgren. op.cit.

[104] Brooks, David. "In Search of Dignity." New York Times, July 7, 2009.

come down to whether he goes to vote after coming from work (he'll vote for A) or goes after seeing his girlfriend (he'll vote for B). Other voters are not so arbitrary, but since there is no right or wrong answer and Warren doesn't have the interest to delve deeply into all the issues, he may just toss a coin. Or, because he committed in public to being a backer of Candidate A in a poker game with his friends, Warren may staunchly back A almost like he backs his favorite football team. Or, because he thinks (or convinces himself) that it doesn't matter who wins, that is, politicians all lie through their teeth, he may abstain from voting, either being honest about it or, possibly, telling his friends or co-workers that he did vote.

An interesting side note to Warren's arbitrary behavior is offered in a recent column by David Brooks.[105] "When you renew your driver's license, you have a chance to enroll in an organ donation program. in countries like Germany and the U.S., you have to check a box if you want to opt in. Roughly 14 percent of people do. But behavioral scientists have discovered that how you set the defaults is really important. So in other countries, like Poland or France, you have to check a box if you want to opt out. In these countries, more than 90% of people participate." Note that the operant variable here is whether or not you will take the time to read the instructions and the trouble to put a check mark in a box! Not whether you want or don't want to donate an organ! While 14% of respondents believe in organ donation enough to check a box, roughly three-quarters of the people would rather donate an organ rather than check a box! If one can decide whether or not to donate an organ based on your tolerance for box-checking, it should come as no surprise that Warren may be arbitrary or vacillate in his voting behavior.

As for, lying or stretching the truth, it usually pays in politics. The self-interest of candidates, served by the self-

[105] Brooks, David. "The Unexamined Society." New York Times Op-Ed, July 7, 2011.

interest of the campaign managers that work for them, and the lobbyists that pay for them, leads to advertisements and statements that are less the truth than they are "what will sell in Peoria." And what sells is not necessarily factual. It is also difficult for politicians to present audiences with unpleasant truths. Tom Friedman implores President Obama to "...set an example and tell the cold, hard truth - to parents and kids [about the sacrifices needed to restore our economy and our leadership position in the world]. Honesty, we are told, is suicidal in politics."[106]

Media, too, can contribute to the confusion. Some fonts of information clearly stem from networks with predisposed biases. Others lean over backwards to not appear biased, even if it means shading the truth. Paul Krugman once "...joked long ago that if one party declared that the earth was flat, the headlines would read 'Views Differ on Shape of Planet.'"[107]

Truthiness, a word coined by Stephen Colbert in 2005,[108] seems to rule the day in politics, as of the Fall of 2008.[109] Truthiness is what a speaker knows in his gut or heart to be true, without regard to whether it makes sense factually. "Proofiness," the title of a 2010 book by Charles Seife points out that numbers hold a particular ability to confuse and bamboozle most of us without a Ph.D. in math. Many of the claims made by politicians are positively "proofy."[110]

---

[106] Friedman, Thomas L. "The Whole Truth and Nothing But." New York Times Op-Ed, September 6, 2011.

[107] Krugman, Paul. "The Centrist Cop-Out." New York Times Op-Ed, July 28, 2011.

[108] From "The Colbert Report." October 17, 2005.

[109] Rich, Frank. "Truthiness Stages a Comeback," New York Times Week In Review, 9/21/2008, p. 9.

[110] Seife, Charles. (2010). op cit.

On occasion, the self-interest of candidates to get elected may lead them directly to lies and/or exaggeration. In a debate held in Iowa on August 11, 2011, the eight candidates were asked "if they would reject a deal to cut the deficit that had 10 times the amount of spending cuts as it had tax increases."[111] "That has been the nature of every Republican debate this cycle: deny the truth or tell and outrageous lie with such bellicosity that no one dares to challenge it. Representative Michele Bachmann, for example, said the credit downgrade was because the government could not pay its debt. Standard and Poor's [the downgrading agency] said it was because lawmakers like her did not take a default seriously. Ron Paul ridiculously claimed that the United States is bankrupt..."[112]

Each of the eight candidates said they would vote against a more than reasonable cut to spending ratio, because that would've got them into trouble with the Tea Party wing of the Republican party. Saying yes would have also made them a target for the other seven on the podium. In effect each of them put their own skin above the best choice for the people of the country. In a way, our Constitution implies that we vote our *Direct* Self-Interest. By making decisions related to keeping their butt in office, some politicians (of both parties) are voting their *Protective* Self-Interest. What would our founding fathers say about that?

As far as Bachmann and Paul taking liberty with the facts, no one in the audience seemed to notice, mind or call them on it; candidates dismiss media attacks as coming from the biases of a "liberal press." The question remains, however, what should or can be done when a candidate outright lies to an audience. Should we, as an electorate, ignore it, or should we demand better from the people who

---

[111] New York Times, editorial, August 12, 2011.

[112] ibid

want us to trust them to lead us? There are no facts any more.[113]

---

[113] For kicks, I looked up President Obama's job approval rating on September 3, 2011 on RCP (Real Clear Politics) which averages seven polls including Gallup and Rasmussen. On average 43.7% of people approved of his job performance, and 51.3% disapproved. I'm rounding to 44 and 51. But what does this really mean?

First, what is the temporal context? If his ratings have been on the rise for the last six or so months, this 44% means something different than if his numbers were greater in previous months. (The latter is true.)

Second, is 44% good for a sitting President in the 11th quarter of his 16 quarters during his first term? Have other Presidents at this point in their tenure done better or worse? (In recent times, only Jimmy Carter has done worse).

Third, how do you factor in the kinds of external and internal stressors that affect the whole U.S. government, and affect each Presidential era differentially, to the approval rating. The general feeling is that the amount of partisanship has reached a new high in Washington (one indication is the dismal approval rating of Congress). If this is a very difficult Congress for a president to deal with, how do you compare his approval ratings to other presidents who have not had to deal with such a situation. The same can be said about wars (Afghanistan, Iraq, Vietnam), natural disasters (Katrina, Irene, Japan earthquake), economic up/downturns (Great Recession of 2008, the jobs crisis and housing crisis that ensued) and terrorist attacks (9/11).

Fourth, shouldn't the ratings of the president's approval be compared to that of other politicians, specifically that of Congress? RCP's numbers for Congress are an awful lot lower than for Obama, with (rounded) 12% approving and 84% disapproving. In this context, Obama seems to be well thought of. A further context, available on RCP is opinions about the direction of the country. 19% think we're going in the right direction, 74% the wrong.

The point is that context is everything. From the initial figure (44% approval), one can make an argument that Obama is doing well compared to other politicians, is doing well considering the within-government and outside of government stressors that have occurred during his presidency, or could argue that his boat is sinking and he is one of the worst presidents we've had in the last 50 years. The numbers can be spun either way.

Even science can become fair game for obfuscation or downright lying.[114] Shulman describes how scientists working for the government have been subject to intimidation with the result that scientific evidence has been suppressed. "The distortion and suppression of science is dangerous, and not just because it means that public money gets wasted on programs, like abstinence-only sex 'education' schemes, that do not work. It is dangerous because it is an assault on science itself, a method of thought and inquiry on which our modern civilization is based and which has been hugely successful as a way of acquiring knowledge that lets us transform our lives and the world around us. In many respects science has been the dominant force - for good and ill - that has transformed human lives over the past two centuries."[115] If politicians, in their own self-interest, can make scientists bend the truth, and the scientists go along because it is in their own self-interest to keep their jobs, how are blokes like you or me or Warren going to serve *our own* self-interests fairly. Odds are we won't. People who sell wrong information based on *their* own self-interest are, in effect, trying to commandeer *our* self-interest.

Paul Krugman, an (admittedly liberal) Op-Ed columnist for the New York Times, points out that the leading aspirants for the Republican nomination in 2012, Rick Perry and Mitt Romney, seemed to deny scientific evidence. Perry stated that evolution is "just a theory" and that climate change is the result of a conspiracy among scientists to direct grant money to themselves. Romney, in his inimitable style hedged, saying that he's not sure that global warming is the result of human action. Both seemed to be pandering to the people of Iowa, only 21% of whom believe in global warming and 35% believe in evolution.

---

[114] Shulman,, Seth. "Undermining Science: Suppression and Distortion in the Bush Administration," University of California Press, 2008.

[115] Judson, Olivia. "Back to Reality" New York Times Online, December 4, 2008.

And to think that one of these men could have been President of the United States! [116][117]

In some ways, we are moving more in the direction of totalitarian regimes, which only release politically "correct," vetted and filtered news. The only difference is that in those regimes there is only one source of inaccurate information, while in our country there are a whole bevy of party lines carrying biased, and therefore unreliable, information. Guess we're just lucky. Al Gore makes the case that the Internet is one possible remedy for this, by moving much of the control of the media from highly funded sources to individuals. The problem is that many Americans are not yet internet-savvy or are so overwhelmed by the amount of available information that they rely on only one site or source. Further, the internet itself is a perfect medium with which to circulate false information.

Something that would help us filter the wheat from the chaff is to be able to isolate unbiased or at least less biased sources of information. We trust an unpoliticized Food and Drug Administration to protect us against harmful remedies and disease-bearing food. We trust rating agencies to assess sex and violence in movies and the safety of toys. Standard & Poors and Moody's are services that provide us with ratings for stocks and bonds, theoretically enabling all investors to play with the same information. They do make mistakes however, as in the financial crisis of 2008, and have a way to go to earn back the respect that was squandered.

Perhaps the time has come for an agency to be devised to assess the biases of the larger sources of news and to require that facts be checked before potentially incendiary information is released to the public. Well-

---

[116] Krugman, Paul. "Republicans Against Science." New York Times Op-Ed, August 28, 2011.

[117] "In The Land of Denial." New York Times Editorial, September 6, 2011.

respected newspapers seem to have established criteria for "going to print" with a story. This model could be expanded to include fact-checking and bias-ratings. Wikipedia, the online encyclopedia, though not bias-free, is relatively clean because it is open to public correction. And on its site, it does describe the biases of certain national television networks; FOX News to the right, MSNBC to the left. Snopes.com has become a source for checking out the truth or falsity of "urban legends" and FactCheck.org is good for seeing that politicos take the high road.

Perhaps new careers of "fact checker," and/or "bias assessor" will gradually develop. As with the job of financial auditor, impartiality and reliance on scientific evidence would be part of the package. People and news sources might still have their agendas, but at least we'd be more aware of them. And while we agree with the right to free speech guaranteed by the First Amendment, we see the need for a parallel right to know if what we are hearing is true, false or just a matter of opinion.

It also seems like a good idea for parents to learn and teach critical thinking. That is, to teach their children how to filter information, how to look for sources and kinds of bias, how to question the veracity of facts and how to seek balance in the information they receive and act on. Schools may help here by emphasizing not only the study of science itself, but the process of scientific thought. Since information sources are more diverse, less monitored and more biased, it will behoove all of us to be more discerning receptors. If we don't, I've got a bridge in Brooklyn that I'd like to sell you...

The international arena is no stranger to the vagaries of self-interest. The political self-interests of the collective population of one nation may be opposed to the self-interests of other peoples. Fifty years ago, if a coal plant in Kansas emitted fumes, no one in China complained. They wouldn't think that they were being adversely affected, even if they knew. Now, if a coal plant in China spews particulates, greenhouse gases and sulfur dioxide, we are affected by both the pollution and the possible climatic effects. It is no longer hidden. We know we are being hosed. Since we, in America, are responsible for about one quarter of the pollution from greenhouse gases being added into the atmosphere, others may very well see *us* as the bad guys. Americans are not used to being in that role. How will we like it, as the 21st century progresses, as China and India become the worst polluters, and we come to see *ourselves* as the victims. We won't be complacent then, but by that time, what they do will be even more out of our control. The sooner we act, when we are, so to speak, on top of the world, the more we can lead by example. The self-interests of America, China and India will almost certainly be in competition with one another.

With globalization comes an increased interdependence and competition between and among nations. This is not necessarily all for the good. Skirmishes between nations, such as the one between the Republic of Georgia and Russia in August of 2008, and global food shortages all lead to increased militarism, protectionism and nationalism. Competition between one nation or region and another, whether military or over resources, works against global cooperation and thus globalism.[118] Bad mortgage loans in one country can have ripple effects throughout the global economy.[119]

David Brooks coined the term "globosclerosis" to describe one large unintended and unwanted side effect of the spread of power.[120] Globosclerosis refers to the paralysis in the ability of willing nations to get anything done on a large-scale basis. As global power becomes increasingly decentralized with the rise of countries like

---

[118] Krugman, Paul. "The Great Illusion," New York Times Op-Ed, August 8, 2008.

[119] Examples are Ireland, Greece and Portugal, among others.

[120] Brooks, David. "Missing Dean Acheson," New York Times Op-Ed, August 1, 2008.

China and India, more nation states can block collective action to solve global problems. "The world has failed to effectively end genocide in Darfur. Chinese and Russian vetoes foiled efforts to impose sanctions on Zimbabwe. The world has failed to implement effective measures to deter Iran's nuclear ambitions. The world has failed to embrace a collective approach to global warming. Europe's drive toward political union has stalled... ...In each case, the logic is the same. Groups with a strong narrow interest are able to block larger groups with a diffuse but generalized interest. The narrow Chinese interest in Sudanese oil blocks the world's general interest in preventing genocide. Iran's narrow interest in nuclear weapons trumps the world's general interest in preventing a Middle East arms race. Diplomacy goes asymmetric and the small defeat the large."[121] [122] The problem, Brooks argues, is that there is no sense of common allegiance as there would be, say, in a democracy. "Everybody feels they have the right to say no, and in a multipolar world, many people have the power to do so. There is no mechanism to wield authority. There are few shared values on which to base a mechanism."[123]

Capitalism, with its built-in competitive engine makes our country great. But other nations have similar beliefs about their own systems and will look out for their own national self-interest. World capitalism, that is competition among nation states, means that we vie for natural and human resources with others. If demand grows for oil worldwide, the price that we have to pay goes up. With

---

[121] ibid

[122] And, it might be added, that small groups with narrow interests and lots of money, can significantly affect the fairness of the outcome of an election in the United States. Witness the "Swift Boaters" in 2004, whose misinformation (though the facts did not come out until after the election) had a serious adverse effect on the Presidential hopes of John Kerry.

[123] op. cit.

labor in Asia and South America cheaper than labor at home, many jobs in the U.S. are lost or outsourced. By bequeathing the manufacturing sector, especially of high-tech products, to overseas competitors, we are increasing the likelihood that some other country may come up with the "next best thing" and we can lose our edge in being the world's innovators.[124] We're still competitive in many areas, but sometimes we lose when we compete. Supply, demand, competition for resources, in fact capitalism, sometimes bites us in our collective American butt. The world isn't simple any more. And it sounds like we're in for a long drawn-out worldwide food fight.

Food fights involving self-interest seem to exist on the home front as well. Expanding on Brooks' idea of globosclerosis, it seems like there is "democracy-sclerosis" also. In the 2008 national election, the Democrats won the White House and both houses of Congress by clear majorities. One would think that would be enough to institute policy changes. Yet major legislative initiatives have been delayed, or watered down, or stalled over and over, whether aimed at fixing health care, rescuing the financial system or eliminating pork from bills that are up for consideration. Each politician has his or her own axe to grind, and our system allows grinding ad libitum. Majority rules turns into super-majority rules. It's almost as if every politician and interest group has a veto over what gets passed, and can hold out their vote until pork, which allows them to give their constituents a gift, is added to a piece of legislation. This played out in real time with the attempt to pass the Affordable Care Act at the end of 2009. Senators from a few states demanded sweetheart deals for their constituents as the price for their vote. When the bill was finally passed, the battle now turns toward ways in which the Republicans can weaken it, delay or repeal it.

---

[124] Shinkle, Kirk. "Is America Losing Its Edge: Giving up on high-tech manufacturing could stifle innovation," interview with Richard Elkus, U.S. News & World Report, 8/18/2008, p. 56.

It was been noted, on a recent radio show, that the election of Senator Scott Brown in Massachusetts seemed to indicate that people were angry with what was going on politically.[125] The host asked listeners to give opinions about who they were angry at. Answers ranged from Obama, to the last administration, to the Democratic Congress, to Republican obstructionism, to the disappointment registered in citizens who expected more rapid solutions to the problems they faced. Looking at it from a Selfonomics point of view, it seems that it is clearly the system that is to blame. The same system that instructs us to pursue our own happiness and to vote our self-interest, is the same system that results in democracy-sclerosis.

Brown's election, left Democrats with "only" 59 out of 100 votes in the Senate. When 41% of the Senate has, in effect, veto power over 59%, is this really rule by majority? It should be noted that the 41 Republican Senators extant at the time of Brown's election represented only 37.3% of the people, since they tend to come from less populous states.[126] Democracy-sclerosis?

The recent Supreme Court decision, which went against a hundred years of precedent, to allow corporations to support causes in national elections, puts an inordinate amount of power and influence into the hands of a select few executives that represent the interests of big business. Again, is this majority rule? Whether one likes or dislikes these results, it should be clear that self-interest, channeled by the rules outlined in our Constitution, is their cause. With the "shellacking" of the Democrats in the 2010

---

[125] From: The Brian Lehrer Show, N.P.R. January 25, 2010.

[126] Calculations used the 2010 census. If a given state had two Republican Senators at that time, the whole population was put in the Republican column. If a state had one Senator from each party, the population of the state was halved and put into the Republican column. Republican Senators represented 112,403,000 out of the U.S. population of 301,366,000 (figures rounded to thousands).

midterm elections, and the resultant Republican majority in the House of Representatives, accomplishing anything has become even more difficult, if that is possible.

An interesting take on the our political system is that, metaphorically, "the American body politic suffers from autoimmune disorders."[127] In effect, the our country, through the Constitution and our body of laws, has within it, the seeds of our own destruction, as does an autoimmune disorder. "The Truthers decided the U.S. government was behind 9/11. Others decided our black president is definitely foreign-born and Muslim. Tea Party Republicans are convinced his administration is crypto-socialist and/or proto-fascist. The anti-Shariah people are terrified of the nonexistent threat of Islamic law infecting American jurisprudence. It's now considered reasonable to regard organs and limbs of the federal government - the E.P.A., the education department, the Federal Reserve - as tumors that must be removed. Taxation itself is now considered a parasitic pathogen rather than a crucial part of our social organism."[128] Our body of laws *allows* this radical desire to purify and dismantle America.

To close this chapter, we will again turn to one of our favorite sources of opinion (and wisdom), David Brooks. The context of his column, "The Grand Bargain Lives!"[129] is the tortuous and torturous runup to the August 2, 2011 deadline by which the national debt limit had to be raised, or the country will default on its obligations. Eleven days before the deadline, Brooks looked at the debate from the perspective of a member of Congress, either Democrat or Republican, examining the issues and motivations that will

---

[127] Andersen, Kurt. "Our Politics Are Sick." New York Times Op-Ed, August 19, 2011.

[128] ibid.

[129] Brooks, David. "The Grand Bargain Lives!" New York Times Op-Ed, July 21, 2011.

guide their actions to support or not to support a "Grand Bargain," defined as one of several vague plans that represent a combination of raising the debt ceiling, cutting spending, and raising revenues. Brooks averred that the rational Congressperson will accept one of these omnibus plans, *for the good of the country*. Italics were added because "for the good of the country" smacks of altruistic-like behavior (which disappears under scrutiny) and ignores self-interest.

From a Selfonomics point of view, even though Grand Bargain was reached and passed through Congress, human nature was being ignored. Using Brooks' words, here are what he says are the influences on the individual Congressperson along with our translation into Selfonomic language (in italics):

"You are being asked to risk your political life for an approach that bears little resemblance to what you would ideally prefer." *I might not get reelected which is certainly not in my self-interest. And I'll be voting for things that I don't believe in, which is also not in my self-interest.*

"You do it because all the other options are worse." *If I am trying to serve my country, voting for the compromise will create less pain for the citizenry than letting us default. Serving my country makes me feel good, so it is in my self-interest to vote for the compromise.*

"You do it [compromise] because even though you are unhappy, you see that people on the other end of the political spectrum are also unhappy." *It is in my self-interest because I can save face knowing that the other side gave in also, and I can see myself as a reasonable and moderate person, which is in my self-interest (except for Tea Party adherents, for whom sticking to their guns is a badge of honor and serves their own self-interest).*

"You do it because both bargains would boost growth." *If I am a Republican, I believe that cutting spending will boost growth, but if I am a Democrat, I believe the opposite, especially if the cuts hit the middle and lower classes hard and go easy on the wealthy. For a Republican, increasing revenues, especially if it is extracted from the wealthy, goes against self-interest, while the opposite holds for Democrats.*

In my opinion, we need to remember the business meeting example from an earlier chapter to best understand this situation. If the reader recalls, the people sitting around the table had widely divergent motives; some wanting to contribute, some wanting to score brownie points or stay out of trouble, some were inattentive and hoping for the meeting to end, and some were intent on playing footsie under the table. The same type of variation in motives will hold for members of Congress. Consider the hypothetical legislators below:

Bob: My primary motivation is to get re-elected. I've worked hard to get to Congress all my life and know   that if I'm not careful, I'll give ammunition to my putative opponent in the next election, which is not that far off. I will vote for compromise only if I'm pretty certain that it will get me re-elected. This is the only career I've ever wanted and I won't throw it away.

Sally: It is not in my best interest to commit to any particular action, until I'm absolutely sure it's the right decision for me. By not committing to any one action, I am protecting myself from making an about face, or angering my base, or giving anyone ammunition against me. If I feel safe I can vote for compromise.

Jim: Maybe the old timers in Congress don't have to worry about re-election, because they are automatic winners in their district or are ready to retire but for me, a first termer, compromise may equate to trouble. As long as I stay true to my base, I'm doing my job.

Sue: I'm finally in a position of leadership in the Congress (Speaker of the House, Majority/Minority leader or Whip). I have to act carefully so I don't put my leadership role in jeopardy. I serve many masters. I need to survive if I am to serve my country.

Gary: I have publicly stated for years that I believe in X. If I appear to change my mind, I will look and feel like a fool. I've been caught in that trap before and won't let it happen again. I need to protect myself from having to explain my actions. I need to be seen as consistent.

Jill: I really believe that sticking to my guns is better for me and my constituents. If I give in, I will be going against the people that elected me. If I stick to my guns and I lose, at least I can hold my head high, while if I sell out I'll be seen as a turncoat.

John: To compromise, I will have to break ranks with kindred spirits in my party. They will feel as if I have deserted them and when I need their support for some issue that is important to me, they might not back me up.

Barbara: I don't like losing, especially to the well-intentioned but misguided ideologues on the other side. I didn't get this far by giving in. I like my reputation of being a bulldog.

Joe: If I hold out until the end, my experience tells me that either the other guy will give in or I'll get a better deal that I've gotten so far. As a Republican, I know that we are more strong willed than the Democrats. They've given in before. (Or as a Democrat, I am sick of compromising with rigid Conservatives. It's time to take a stand. Plus, I always loved a good poker game.)

Ann: I've always believed in the Lord. He helped me to get where I am and I'm not going to let him down by giving in to the other side. They can say what they want, but I'm being true to him.

Ten "types" of motivation, each slightly different are represented above. The reader can, I'm sure, think of more. And it is likely that various combinations of these prototypes exist in other legislators. One person may feel good being loyal to their constituency and doing the work of God. Another might pride herself on being a good but tough negotiator who is willing to compromise for the good of the country. The point is that there are sure to be a wide variety of self-interests sitting in the Chambers of Congress. To assume that the same noble intentions motivate all of them is surely a mistake.

While the reader may think this analysis is too cynical, if it weren't fairly accurate, wouldn't the arguments over the debt ceiling, spending cuts and increased revenue be settled more easily? If the pressures on the people in Congress were as Brooks described, wouldn't compromises already have been made? Who is served by letting the clock tick down to the last second? The people of our nation? Certainly not. The World Markets? No. The only people who benefit (or avoid negative consequences) by inaction, are individual politicians, each looking out for their own self-interest.

CHAPTER 15: SELF-INTEREST AND RELIGION

Religion has existed, in various forms, in just about every society, in every country, in every age. That makes sense if one assumes an all-knowing, all-powerful God, that humans, at all points in time, in every place on the planet, worship. But that's not quite the case. First, there are members of some religions that say that their belief system is the correct one and that all others are wrong. That makes the rest of us heathens, even though we believe in God in our own way. Second, if some cultures worship animals, others worship the sun and moon, or idols, or one God, or many, how can so many people be wrong if one culture is right?

Although belief in some sort of religion seems to be universal, there may be an underlying concept that can explain both that universality and the differences and disagreements in the object and flavor of that worship. What can explain everything is self-interest.

Nicholas Wade sees [130]religion as having evolved culturally in the same manner as physical characteristics. "The ancestral human population of 50,000 years ago, to judge from living hunter-gatherers, would have lived in small egalitarian groups without chiefs or headmen. Religion served them as an invisible government. It bound people together, committing them to put their community's needs ahead of their own self-interest. For fear of divine punishment, people followed rules of self-restraint toward members of the community. Religion also emboldened them to give their lives in battle against outsiders. Groups fortified by religious belief would have prevailed over those

---

[130] Wade, Nicholas. "Evolution of the God Gene." New York Times, November 15, 2009.

that lacked it, and genes that prompted the mind toward ritual would eventually have become universal."

An additional raison d'être for religion is simply man's mortality. As Ben Franklin said, nothing is certain but death and taxes. From our perspective, we can't do anything about taxes, but death is another story. What if we could wangle our way to immortality? What if we could minimize the pain and sadness that we feel here on earth and lessen the dread of actually dying, by thinking that our time here on earth is just a fraction of our lives, and therefore, not that important? Wouldn't believing in an afterlife be in our best interest? Not just you and me, but *everyone who has ever lived*?

Notice that it is in our individual self-interest to believe in a God or another supreme being, *whether or not there actually is one.* As a matter of fact, whether or not there is a God may be close to irrelevant. It's the *belief* in God that serves our self-interest, not necessarily the *existence* of God. Not many of us have encountered God, or had our wishes and prayers answered on more occasions than what would be expected statistically by chance. But the great majority of us have gotten comfort from the belief in the existence of God. The belief in God allows us to know that someone close to us, who is dying, or has just died, is going to or has gone to a better place, that he or she will be close to God, and that our own death is more than just nothingness.

But what of the organized religions, with their millions of (mostly) men who lead or represent the various iterations of God and their billions of followers? Does it mean that it's all a charade, and that we're all fooling ourselves? Maybe. Maybe not. If God does exist, then religions and their trappings all make sense. Could all these structures and systems of people and beliefs that make up religion have come about if God does *not* exist? Yes. Read on…

It's 35,000 years ago, approximately 33,000 B.C. Grod lived in an agricultural community with his extended family somewhere on the Eurasian continent. His group, or tribe, consisted of about 100 people, divided into perhaps 15 interrelated families. Life was hard, but the hardest thing for any of the tribe to deal with was when a family member got sick and died. Or just died, killed by a local carnivore, or member of a nearby rival tribe. Grod, an elder of his tribe, at 35 years of age, wanted to soften the blow for the rest of his family and tribe, when his brother Cred died while hunting for food.

Grod somehow made a mental connection between people who lived and died here on the land (there was no concept of "Earth") and the points of light that appeared frequently in the evening sky (there was not concept of "stars" either). He suggested to his brother's widow and her children that when Cred died he became one of those points of light that one could see in the sky. Cred could look down on his wife and children, and they could glance up and see him and feel a connection.

It did make Cred's family feel better and less alone. It also gave them the message that when they too died, they would not just cease to exist, but would join their father in the sky. Grod was esteemed within his tribe for his "discovery," and was given a special place in the tribe, that of a "Seer." Passed down over generations within this tribe, the story of dying and going into the sky became more elaborate. A person within the community was designated as the Seer and would help grieving relatives adjust to the death of loved ones and their eventual own demise.

As the original tribe came into contact with other tribes over centuries and millennia, the concept of the Seer caught on and spread, because it now served a vital purpose within all the communities that it touched. And as tribes merged, reformed and split up, slightly different conceptions of the Seer legend emerged, much like the way the "telephone game" changes a story through retelling it (this time with a higher purpose).

What the various versions of the legend had in common is that life did not end here on earth. There was an eternal afterlife, during which people who died on earth went up into the sky, or heavens. The part of them that ascended was called the "soul" which was invisible and intangible, unlike the bones of the deceased that remained on earth. Over time, the position and function of the Seer became integral to all human communities and the purview of the position expanded. The Seer in each community, was a teacher of right and wrong, using access to the sky, or "heaven," as a carrot (and sometimes banishment from heaven as a stick), in some cases an emissary of a divine being, eventually called God, who created the natural world. The one that had the answers to unanswerable questions.

For example, why do some tribe members die when young, and yet others live to a ripe old age? The answers varied from "It's God's will," to "God needs the good ones to live with him," to "We're being tested." Behaving well in this world meant a pleasant afterlife. Behaving poorly meant guilt and the threat of eternal damnation. Belief in the Seer and the God he represented was one important means of keeping a lid on the self-interest of tribe members who, if left to their own devices, might rob and kill each other.

Over the centuries, the Seers became priests and imams and monks and rabbis, and their preaching became various brands of religion. While they all had a common original purpose, that is, to explain events such as death that were otherwise inexplicable, the explanations varied enough to create different sects with slightly different belief systems which, over centuries, diverged even further. All the religions of the world were established before man knew anything about disease, or science, or in fact, that the earth was not flat. The Seers and Priests were primitive men, with scant knowledge. They derived their power from the needs, the self-interests, of the people they served.

Not many of us are comfortable with the idea of nothingness after death. We want to believe in something, and the Seers give us that story. We are taught religious beliefs as youngsters. Those beliefs become central to our thought process and are quite resistant to change as we get older. They are cast in stone, not only because they were taught to us when young, but because they deal with monumental issues, and offer acceptable answers to impossible problems.

So when we are taught that our religion is the best, we don't question it. If we're taught that other religions don't quite have the right answer, we don't question that either. Four hundred to five hundred years ago, religious wars were common on the European continent. They were possible because people believed their religious leaders that told them that the better life waited for them in heaven, after their life ended here on earth. If one really believes that, then dying for your faith is not such a bad thing. In fact, it might score more points in heaven.

Religion and its Seers serves our self-interest well. First, it provides answers to questions that we, despite the advances of science over the last couple of centuries, still cannot answer. Second, it allows us to have a feeling of belonging to a group which, for many of us, is a good thing. Third, it serves our PSI, or protective self-interest, extremely well by ensuring that we will achieve salvation after death. All we have to do is play by the rules of our religion. It also helps us to "hedge our bets," in that there is nothing lost if God does not exist. If he does, then we're on the right side. And of course, belief allows us to be at peace more when we die. It is surely more appealing to think that when we die we will see our parents and other loved ones in heaven, than to think that everything will just end.

It is to be remembered, however, that the Seers, the ones who pass on the religion from generation to generation, are just human. This means that they operate in their own self-interest, just as people do in economic situations. In previous chapters we came across different sets of people that looked out for themselves by playing within the rules, or laws. The Seers are no different. They take their religious beliefs as dogma, and logically come to conclusions about the way people should think and behave.

Additionally, they have a vested interest in their own particular brand of religion, because that is where their status and expertise derives from. Their legitimacy comes through their mission and their brand name. And, of course, their beliefs in God make *their* time on earth and *their* demise more comfortable also. It's a win-win; helping others and themselves at the same time.

Each religion must rationalize its own importance, just as mortgagors, mortgagees and stock brokers do. But it's a much easier sell. They are serving the public interest, or they are not doing any harm, they are helping people to cope with life, they are doing God's work. Each Seer's own life is dependent on others believing in what he or she preaches. The religion gives the Seer a job, gives them status and power within the community. To the extent that there are others who have a different view on religion, or don't believe at all, that is a threat to their "business." So the Seers have a vested interest in their perception of things, their religion, their sect.

It's easy to envision a situation similar to that described above that differs only in the source ascribed to eternal life. If a person, similar to Grod, at a different place and time, points to cows, or idols or large trees as a representation of the continuity of life, and it serves to comfort the relatives of the deceased, that group may end up worshipping cows, idols or large trees or, theoretically, all living things. Dealing with the inexplicability and certainty of eventual death is the motivator for belief in religion.

In sum, what all humans have in common is mortality. Death and dying are beyond our understanding, so that we need a set of beliefs to ease our suffering, our loss of loved ones and the idea of our own demise. Religion fills those needs, whether God exists or does not. This explanation is *not* anti-religion or anti-God. It is apart from religion. Given self-interest as the prime mover, belief in God and religion makes sense. Let's face it, anyone or any belief system that offers the hope of eternal life is going to be pretty popular.

Religion brings us comfort and solace, gives us answers to the unanswerable and allows us to feel like we belong to a larger group of people. Unfortunately, it also creates antipathy between and among people and peoples. It is too often seen as zero sum; that is, if you're right, I'm wrong. If your God exists, then mine doesn't. If you are righteous, I'm a heathen. And so religion can be a unique source of strength for humanity, or be a font of exquisite pain and suffering.

CHAPTER 16: PROBLEMS CREATED BY TECHNOLOGY

Self-interest is intimately woven into the fabric of societal values. In 2007, a conference at Yale university convened to discuss human alienation from nature and how it is related to our consumerism and materialism.[131] Although the goals of the conference were certainly laudable, self-interest may preclude achieving them.   For example, one issue pointed out, that "Humans have grown too apart from the natural world," is hard to argue with, especially as many of our family members have their fingers flying over the keyboard of some electronic device as you read this. On the other hand why would we want to spend more time outdoors? How do you get people to give up air conditioning in their homes and cars? Would you? Or to agree to not watch television, use computers, or cook with electric appliances. For the great majority of the population, being outside and "communing with nature" is much more appealing in thought than in action, of course with occasional exceptions.

In order to get people outside, it has to work for *them*. Has to "move" them. Two easy-to-sell reasons for being outside are keeping healthy and sightseeing. Running, hiking, bird-watching, photography and beautiful scenery may all be motivators. For those of us for whom outside activities are of little interest, we may venture out occasionally, especially when the weather cooperates, but

---

[131]In 2007 (October 11-14), the Yale School of Forestry and Environmental Studies chaired a conference entitled "Toward a New Consciousness: Values to Sustain Human and Natural Communities," in Aspen, Colorado (Anthony A. Leiserowitz and Lisa O. Fernandez, with a Forward by James Gustave Speth and an Afterword by Stephen R. Kellert. Copies freely available at www.yale.edu/environment/publications

we won't give up our electronics and controlled temperatures for nineteenth century living conditions.

Technology, especially, can be a catalyst to a person's individual self-interest. It enabled this author to become *the* world expert on a rather obscure topic in no time. My mother, Doris Tauber Gribin, was a songwriter who lived from 1908 to 1996 and wrote the melody to a famous song entitled "Them There Eyes." Since 2000, I have been able to amass roughly 400 different renditions of this song on computer, a raft of graphics about the singers of these versions, and many articles about the composers and performers of this song. This achievement could not have been close to possible without the internet. Other wonks, with different passions could fairly quickly become world-class micro-experts on subjects as compelling as the history of sport-top bottles, television clickers, or folk art in southwestern Topeka, Kansas.

As far as I can tell, this is technology having a good effect on my self-interest, although after the first couple of hundred times I heard the song, I began to wonder. Technology is moving so fast, there's a good chance that we have no idea how self-interest will be affected or channeled. We have the ability to do business with, talk to, and befriend someone on the other side of the earth, in real time. As we are more in touch with people far away, we are less in touch with people closer to us. Time is zero sum, so we can't be talking to our neighbor over the back fence if we're speaking with someone in Europe over Skype. If humans can follow our self-interests via different paths than a generation ago, how will that affect individuals and/or society?

There is also a distinct dilution of influences, interests and sources of information. In the 1950s and 1960s, there were a limited number of radio and television stations, newspapers and magazines. Every kid in your class watched the same popular sitcoms ("I Love Lucy," "Mash," "All In The Family," "Seinfeld," "Friends") and parents would be limited to a few newspapers and television stations for sources of news and information. Nowadays, every person has his own experience on the web; millions of websites to visit, hundreds of TV channels and movies from which to choose, and individualized radio stations in the form of iPods. The way we experience the world is becoming more and more individual and diverse. Theoretically we could have more in common with someone across the planet than with our next-door neighbor. We might feel a lot closer to a person, whoever he is, and wherever she is from, if we participate in the same chats, listen to the same music, and interact regularly over a social networking site such as Facebook. Whether we really have things in common is a different story, and perhaps an unnecessary question to even pursue.

Unintended consequences of the rapid spread and dilution of information is that there is less monitoring for accuracy, less control by reputable agencies, and it is harder to assign responsibility to the source of that information. While these are not necessarily bad for humankind, they are not necessarily good either. Consider the Facebook and MySpace phenomena. Are relationships formed on these sites "real," or fantasies, or something in between? They certainly feed self-interest, else they wouldn't be so popular, but will likely change the way we look at friendship. The ties are concurrently weak and intense. You know everything that the people in your circle are doing, and they know everything about *you*.

These services allow "hooking up" through texting, pornography and gambling as people vote with their keystrokes which, in turn, are driven by the self-interest of the keystroker. These services can have significant psychological and social effects on the individual using them. They can feed or destroy egos, make or break relationships, preclude or invite isolation. "Face time" may soon be replaced with "Facebook time." Good? Bad? What will the limits be? How will mankind and society be changed? No one knows.

How will these trends affect the way we raise our kids? There is an implication that as generations progress, our children may have less and less in common with us, their parents, because they are going (electronically) to places that we have trouble grasping. In effect, the self-interests of parents and children may diverge faster than ever before. This may argue for keeping them close to us and monitoring or controlling where they go on the net (although over-control may leave them at an informational and technical disadvantage to peers who are given free rein). The problem with monitoring is that often we, the parents, don't know what we are doing and they, the kids, do. When it comes to computer-wiseness, we're the children and they're the adults.[132] What does that mean for the composition of the family? Again, who knows?

While some of the effects of technology on self-interest are unknown, but not necessarily nefarious, there are others that are clearly undesirable. A person following their self-interest can do an inordinate amount of damage to another person, or other groups of people. Someone with a vendetta against Congressperson John Doe could do a lot of damage to Doe's political career through lies sent in mass email campaigns and might escape consequence.

A recent example of this is found in the 2011 attacks on the Chairman of the Federal Reserve, Ben Bernanke, by candidates for the Republican Presidential nomination, Rick Perry and Michele Bachmann.[133] Perry said that Bernanke's monetary policy was "almost treacherous - or treasonous, in my opinion" and stated that the Fed should be "transparent so that the people of the United States know what they are doing." Bachmann asserted that the Fed's policy was opaque and intimated that the Fed was

---

[132] Blow, Charles M. "A Profile of Online Profiles," New York Times, Op-Ed, September 9, 2009.

[133] Stewart, James B. "Lots of Vitriol for Fed Chief, Despite Facts." New York Times, September 2, 2011.

"printing money," which is economic-speak for inviting inflation. The problem is that all of these accusations are baseless, according to well-respected economists. The skinny is that the Fed did a masterful job of steering us through a very difficult economic time, that it is as transparent as possible (it puts out weekly minutes of its meetings) and is in no way "printing money" or courting inflation. Yet there are very few criticisms of the accusers, even though both the tone of their comments are disrespectful and the content dead wrong.

The immediacy and omnipresence of our media, which can carry this sort of misinformation would have been impossible for the founders of our Constitution to understand and predict. Technology like this didn't exist when they walked the earth.[134]

We, as the audience, need to improve the way we filter this information, to be wary of the sources (similar to the old adage "Don't take candy from a stranger.") and to verify the information pushed at us at fact-checking places like snopes.com. It does seem, however, that we'll always be playing catchup; that is, reacting to rumors rather than being able to prevent them.

Technology allows someone with particular self-interests to legally obfuscate financial arrangements, to affect people around the world financially and politically, to stretch the truth or lie outright about the policies or intentions of political candidates and to prey on people with less sophistication. Some generic examples:

Technology has allowed for complicated financial products, such as "derivatives," formed by bundling individual mortgages together into large units so that shares in these

---

[134] See Collins, Gail. "A Right to Bear Glocks?" New York Times, Op-Ed, January 9, 2011. The column, about the shooting of Gabrielle Giffords, points out that up until recently, political assassinations did not take the lives of innocent bystanders. "The difference is not about the Second Amendment. It's about a technology the founding fathers could never have imagined."

units can be sold.   No one seems to know exactly what is in these bundled products. This product contributed to meltdown in the mortgage and banking sectors in 2008. The stock markets of the world are inextricably linked. Partly because of globalization, but also due to advanced computer technology. When the U.S. market fell precipitously in the Fall of 2008, so did the rest of the markets across the globe.

The 2008 Presidential primaries and the race itself were guided by technology. Huge amounts of money for both major candidates was raised over the internet. Candidates can and did "target" their markets in swing states. Advanced editing and production techniques allowed "stretching the truth" about positions on the issues and implied wrongdoing that in other settings would be seen as slander. Lies, rumors and exaggerations were all spread net-wide with impunity.

Using the internet, people can prey on youngsters, spread rumors about corporations and sell short to profit on the downward spiral of a share price, or bilk elders out of money on phony drug, insurance or miracle health cure offers.

Google, as of 2009, gets 71% of the search activity. This can translate to enormous power if searches are not "neutral;" i.e. "search engines should have no editorial policies other than that their results be comprehensive, impartial and based solely on relevance."[135] The result of non-neutrality may be to harm the self-interest of competitors to Google or its allies, either based on financial or political biases.

---

[135] Raff, Adam. "Search, but You May Not Find." New York Times Op-Ed, December 27, 2009.

The power of the self-interest of one person or a small group of people can be multiplied geometrically by technology. This multiplier effect can be catastrophic for the self-interest of others. Tom Friedman speaks to this point. "Let's not fool ourselves. Whatever threat the real Afghanistan poses to U.S. national security, the 'Virtual Afghanistan' now poses just as big a threat. The Virtual Afghanistan is the network of hundreds of jihadist Web sites that inspire, train, educate and recruit young Muslims to engage in jihad against America and the West. Whatever surge we do in the real Afghanistan has no chance of being a self-sustaining success, unless there is a parallel surge — by Arab and Muslim political and religious leaders — against those who promote violent jihadism on the ground in Muslim lands and online in the Virtual Afghanistan."[136]

Technology seems to be involved in the developmental stages resulting in a number of terrorist attacks in late 2009. Both the plot to blow up an American airliner on Christmas day and the mass murder carried out by and American psychiatrist in Fort Hood, Texas, seem to have been traced to charismatic Muslim clerics. "Internet imams from the Middle East to Britain offer a televangelist's persuasive message of faith, purpose and a way forward, for both the young and as yet uncommitted, as well as for the most devout worshipers ready to take the next step, to jihad..."[137] It is thought that these Imams function as "talent scouts," passing along willing recruits to those that fund, plan and operationalize attacks.

The takeaway seems to be that the self-interest of all of us has been, is and will be affected by the onslaught of technology. It can help people to more easily and effectively pursue their goals, regardless of whether those

[136] Friedman, Tom. "www.jihad.com." New York Times, Op-Ed, December 16, 2009.

[137] Schmitt, Eric and Lipton, Eric. "Focus on Internet Imams as Al Qaeda Recruiters." New York Times, December 31, 2009.

goals are helpful to, neutral to, or anathema to the rest of humanity. And in many cases. we just have no idea what the effects will be until after the fact.

CHAPTER 17: COMPETING SELF-INTERESTS AND "ENTITLEMENTS"

The interest in cutting back on spending to reduce the growing national debt has been fomenting for years. It has been made more urgent by the "Great Recession of 2008" and the midterm elections of 2010, which sent a large number of new congresspersons to Washington that espouse the "Tea Party" philosophy, meaning smaller government and spend-as-you-go fiscal policies. Democrats too, have jumped on the bandwagon, in an attempt to develop fiscally responsible spending, living "within our means" and not "kicking the can down the road." The only disagreement, albeit a huge one, is how to accomplish this.

Lurking in the background are the differing philosophies of the two major parties. The Democrats believe that a combination of spending cuts and an increase in taxes, especially on the wealthy, is the correct path to fiscal responsibility. Republicans believe that any tax hikes will be detrimental to business activity and will slow the economy. In general, Republicans believe that if you put money into the hands of people at the top of the socioeconomic scale they will invest it or put it to work in other ways that will result in a "trickle down" of wealth to those lower on the scale. Democrats believe that by putting money in the hands of the less well-off will result in greater consumer spending which will make money "trickle up" to business owners and investors.

According to the Center on Budget and Policy Priorities, the Federal Government spends about three and a half trillion dollars a year. Roughly 20% is spent on Social Security, 21% on Medicare, Medicaid and aid to children (together called "entitlements"), 14% on other social safety net programs, 20% Defense and Security, 6%

for interest on the national debt, and 19% on miscellaneous items, which includes spending on education, foreign aid, scientific research, infrastructure and benefits to retired federal employees and veterans. This miscellany is sometimes called "discretionary spending."

In order to decrease overall spending, the cuts can't just be made in discretionary spending because it's just not large enough to accommodate substantial enough amounts. That leaves defense and the major entitlements as targets for paring. While Republicans seem more eager than the Democrats to cut entitlements,[138] Democrats are coming around to that view also, though with less enthusiasm and a duller knife.

All of the possible actions surrounding spending cuts are rife with self-interest of individuals, occupational groups, industries, political parties and the politicians themselves. Some of these self-interests are obvious, such as the desire of members of Congress to support the needs of their constituencies, but others are more subtle.

Let's look at the attempt to cut spending for entitlements, primarily Medicare and Medicaid. Much of the following analysis also applies to the Health Care Bill that was passed by Congress in 2010 since the players are the same. Let's start with the citizen who, whether poor, disabled, old or some combination of the three has a lot of "skin in the game" literally and figuratively. Some expressions of their self-interest:

1)   I've worked hard all of my life, I deserve to get the
         best medical treatment.
2)   If I don't look out for myself, who will?

---

[138] Lofgren has pointed out that Democrats "do not understand language." They refer to Social Security and Medicare as "entitlements," a word often associated with getting something not deserved, as with a spoiled child. He suggests calling them "earned benefits" because that is what they actually are. Republicans are much better at messaging; i.e. Obamacare, Patriot Act and Death Tax. See Lofgren, op.cit.

3) My friend Jay had a hip replacement. Why shouldn't I?
4) I'm just as important as the next guy.
5) I'm afraid that if I don't get treated, I'll die.
6) My doctor told me I need those tests.
7) I don't have that much time left. If this therapy or surgery will help me make the most of life, I want it.
8) As long as my insurance (medicare/medicaid/private insurance) will pay for it, I want it.

This will sound crass, but the needs of patients, or patients looking out for *themselves* are almost irrelevant. Yes, other people will care about taking care of the indigent, but that is altruism, and we've talked about that before. It is ephemeral, and disappears under scrutiny. *What makes the needs of patients, or their ISI relevant is whether or not it is correlated with the needs of service groups, such as physicians, nurses and attorneys.* First consider physicians...

A story broadcast on National Public Radio on October 8, 2009 that shed some light on the down-low nature of self-interest. The show was "All Things Considered," the hosts Melissa Block and Michele Norris, the interviewer Alix Spiegel, the title of the story "The Telltale Wombs of Lewiston, Maine." Reacting to the incongruous difference in frequency of certain operations in various towns, a public health physician, Dr. Jack Wennberg did some investigating. In Lewiston, Maine, an inordinate percentage of women were having hysterectomies. He statistically eliminated differences in the health of the populations of various towns, leaving doctors to drive the usage of medical services, rather than patients. Here's part of the interview:

Spiegel: One of the many doctors I talked to while I was in Maine was an eye specialist named Frank Read, another doc from the study groups. He told me this story.

Dr. Read: My old partner that I joined here in 1971 was asked by a friend of his, you know, at what level of vision do you do a cataract operation? And he said, well, if there's one ophthalmologist in town, it's 20/200.

Spiegel: 20/200 is pretty bad vision.

Dr. Read: If there are two ophthalmologists in town, it's 20/80.

Spiegel: Not so bad.

Dr. Read: If there are three ophthalmologists in town, it's 20/40.

Spiegel: Pretty good vision, actually. In other words, when there are more doctors, surgery is being done on patients that are less sick. According to later work done by Jack Wennberg, the number of doctors in a town can influence the amount of medical services consumed across the board. If there's one doctor in a town with 100 patients, then he might schedule your heart checkups for once every six months. If another doctor comes to town, and now the first doctor has 50 patients, he'll just schedule your heart checkups for once every three months for a very simple reason, Frank Read says.

Dr. Read: I don't want to be sitting on my thumbs all the time. I want to be busy. And that may unconsciously loosen my criteria for doing a particular procedure.

Spiegel: Which brings us finally to the subject which incredibly was never, ever directly discussed during the nearly 20 years the doctors met: money, the way money affects medical decisions. Frank Read and Bob Keller told me that this subject was completely verboten.

Dr. Keller: We didn't want to talk about money. That's something that we wouldn't want to acknowledge because it would have been a showstopper. I mean, it would have then gone right to the question of greed, and you're not going to keep a doc at the table if you say you're greedy.

Spiegel: Doctors are uncomfortable acknowledging the role of money, but every person I talked to admitted it affected medical decision-making, including Gordon Smith, head of the Maine Medical Association.

Dr. Smith: Of course, it does. That's just common sense. That's human nature. The payment system is an important influence.

Spiegel: As you might know, most of the doctors in this country are not on salary but are paid basically like pieceworkers in a clothing factory. It's called fee for service. And the way this affects their behavior is clear.

Dr. Smith: If you pay people more the more things they do, they're going to do more things.

Spiegel: And not all kinds of services are paid the same. See, on the most basic level, your doctor is either thinking, talking, advising you, or doing something to you, the procedure. For years, public health experts have agreed that when doctors have the time to do stuff like counsel you about your health behaviors, keep track of your medications, it's better for patients. Still, between talking and procedures, there is no question about which activity is better rewarded by our current payment system.

Dr. Smith: Procedures. Procedures. That produces revenue.

Spiegel: And the more complicated the procedure, the higher the payment. Makes sense. But it has this unintended effect on care. Bob Keller points to his own specialty. He's a back doctor and says that one of the most frequently done operations among back doctors these days is this complicated and pretty expensive procedure called an instrumented spinal fusion. When a patient has degenerative disk disease, the doctor can go in and insert medal rods. Keller says in the old days, doctors used a much simpler and safer operation, but the more complicated one has a clear advantage for doctors.

Dr. Keller: The surgeons could charge more because they were doing these complicated procedures. And so they were putting the screws in. They bill for putting the screws in. They were putting the plates in. They bill for putting the plates in - doing all these things. So you had a whole new high-tech procedure that was enormously attractive to spine surgeons, and it literally took off in this country. At the same time, as most good spine surgeons will admit, they had no research to support what they were doing.

Spiegel: In fact, says Keller, one of the few high-quality studies that did exist showed it wasn't so positive.

Dr. Keller: It showed that it isn't so great, actually, as people thought it was. And they also showed that interestingly enough, that the old-fashioned, non-instrumented fusion was as successful as the instrumented fusion, which was a real blow.

Spiegel: So it's pretty clear that doctors exist in a fee-for-service system that encourages, and really, because of malpractice and having to battle insurance companies, in some ways, actually forces them to do more, more and more complicated surgeries, more elaborate tests, more stuff of every kind. But while most Americans just assume that more care is good, it turns out more isn't always better for patients.

So physicians have skin in the game too, figuratively. The more procedures they do, the more tests they order, the more prescriptions they write, the more money they make. This is especially true if the patient has good insurance. The ISI of the physician and the ISI of the patient to stay as healthy as possible are very highly correlated. Patients almost always want their doctors to err on the side of safety, which may include many MRIs, CAT scans and subsequent back operations, hip and knee replacements, balloon angioplasties or hysterectomies. If the fee that they are allowed to charge per procedure is limited by insurance, the doctor might just do more procedures. The doctors feel good because they are taking extra good care of their patients, while making well-deserved money and avoiding malpractice claims at the same time.[139]

Related professions, such as nursing, have a cost-benefit matrix that is correlated with those of physicians. They want to take the best care of patients as they can, but they also want to ensure that nurses are in demand so salaries stay high and they want to avoid malpractice suits as well.

Attorneys too, play a substantial role here. By fighting against limiting the size of medical malpractice awards, they keep the doctors ordering more procedures to cover their own potential culpability. The lawyers can say that they are just helping clients who are injured by poor medical practice to be compensated for their loss. That is, they are helping see that justice is done. And, incidentally, their own ISI is served by earning higher fees.

Now consider the pharma industry and their myriad of employees. Researchers feel they are doing humanity a service by developing new drugs, and they certainly are. They are also earning their paychecks, serving their own ISIs. The thousands of drug reps have similar incentives to convince doctors that their product is better than its competitors. The management is responsible to the shareholders of the corporation and needs to make a profit. So drugs, until they go generic after (usually) between 7 and 12 years, are quite expensive, driving up the cost of health care. How much profit is enough? As much as possible, the argument being that the more a

---

[139] If doctors can and do look out for themselves when deciding what to do for and with their patients, it's quite likely that other service providers, be they lawyers, plumbers or car mechanics do the same thing. If lawyers are being paid by the hour, they will probably work more hours on your case. Plumbers and mechanics may recommend fixes that may or may not need making.

company makes, the more they can pour back into research to develop new drugs in the long and regulated pipeline.

So far, the ISIs of patients, physicians, nurses, attorneys and drug companies are all highly correlated. Do hospitals fall into the same category? Not necessarily. They are generally *not* in business to make huge profits for shareholders. They are more in the business of passing along costs, so they can provide good care to patients while serving their community and staying afloat financially.

Insurance companies, though usually seen as villains, are similar to hospitals in that they pass costs along. They assess how much they will have to pay out and then add a certain percent for their own profit. They usually place limits on the fees they will pay out per procedure and per diagnosis, but if more procedures are being performed, they have to pay out more money. Then they pass along these cost increases by raising rates. Many of them are publicly held companies, that are obligated to make as much profit as possible for their shareholders.

Returning to the attempt to cut spending, it's an uphill slog, since the self-interest of most of the involved parties are correlated and work *against* cutting the number of services or fees and the rest (hospitals and insurance companies) are neutral to the cuts. Unfortunately, the ISIs of this group of people (patients + doctors + nurses + attorneys), let's call them "Benefiters," goes against the ISIs of all non-Benefiters. It seems to be a zero sum game, in the sense that if you benefit, I lose and vice versa.

The more the Benefiters benefit, the higher the costs of health care to us all, the more you and I pay for health insurance, the less we have to spend on other things, the less other businesses take in from our decreased consumer spending, the more businesses fail, the more people go on unemployment, the higher the cost to governments for providing a safety net for its citizens.

While there are no apparent easy solutions the deficit problem, there are guidelines that can be offered given the inextricable involvement of self-interest:

1) The ISIs of all interested parties must be taken into account and perhaps manipulated. Former White House Advisor on Health Policy, Zeke Emanuel, made this argument in a recent television interview.[140] He noted that 70% of health care costs go to treating chronic illnesses such as diabetes, cancers, chronic pain and emphysema and that any reduction in the cost of health care has to focus on prevention and more efficient treatment in these areas. Using chronic back pain as an example, he cited the overuse of MRIs and too-frequent back surgeries as not only being expensive, but not helping the patient in most cases. (Physical therapy is more effective and should almost always be tried first.) The net-net is that none of these changes will occur, until and unless, the incentive structure for physicians and related parties changes.

2) Since the "game" is zero sum over our entire population, it is only fair that everyone be asked to sacrifice.

3) Those who have more should sacrifice more. Using a Social Security example is easiest. If my monthly payment is $2000/mo and someone else gets $1000 per mo., a 5% cutback affects me more than him. Unfortunately the translation of these cutbacks to health services is much more complicated and the Social Security system is in better shape financially anyway.

4) All changes should be enacted gradually, to ease the "shock to the system" and allow for midcourse corrections. Using the same example, the first year of cuts could be 1% per person, second year 2%, etc., up to 5%. Raising the

---

[140] "Morning Joe," hosted by Joe Scarborough and Mika Brzesinski, on MSNBC, August 31, 2011.

age to receive full benefits would have a similar effect. If one must be 66 to collect full benefits, next year make it 66 years and one month. Increase by one month per year up until twelve years, when the age for full benefits would be 67.

5) As for cutting spending on health care, everything devolves back to the cost of health care itself. "Unless we get health care inflation under control by replacing the perverse fee-for-service incentive structure, there will be no money for anything else."[141] Without somehow changing the incentives of physicians and related groups, so that their ISIs are more highly correlated with the needs of the population in general, there will be no lasting or significant changes. Paul Krugman makes a similar argument, without using the concept of ISI, when talking about the banker class, "This is a negative-sum game, in which the attempt to protect the [medical community] from any losses is inflicting much larger losses on everyone else. "[142]

Any solutions will almost surely have to involve increasing the supply of health care personnel, especially since demand will likely increase with the phase-in of the provisions of the new health care law. Some thoughts along those lines are to fund the training of more doctors, more nurses and especially those intermediate professions of physician's assistant and nurse practitioner. If there are more extant service providers, competition should force down the price of receiving health care.

This also plays nicely with the new Health Care reform act, which will provide coverage to millions of as-yet uncovered individuals which will in turn create a tremendous need for more health care providers. Or perhaps, incenting physicians to hire and supervise PAs and NPs, so that they would be providing more of the

---

[141] Brooks, David. "Pundit Under Protest." New York Times, Op-Ed, June 14, 2011.

[142] "Rule by Rentiers." New York Times. Op-Ed, June 10, 2011.

hands-on care and the physician would be more of a consultant. It's similar to the old adage about teaching someone to farm instead of providing food. For attorneys, limiting medical malpractice awards would lessen the need for physicians to "CYA" by ordering more tests, procedures and expensive drugs.

In sum, self-interest appears to be all-pervasive, frequently goes unrecognized by those exerting it, and is very difficult to admit and talk about. And if we can admit it to ourselves, we have tried and true justifications and rationalizations for our behavior, similar to the ones expressed by physicians in the NPR interview, such as, "He needed that operation." "Better safe than sorry." "If I don't operate, the next guy will." We all wear "self-interest colored glasses."

PART V: SOLUTIONS

Problems arise when the self-interest of one person, group or nation is in conflict with the self-interest of another person, group or nation. One thing that can be tried is to better align the self-interests of the parties that disagree, which may turn a zero-sum situation into a win-win situation. Further, the self-interest of an individual can be better aligned with the interest of the nation or world as a whole.

Changing the rules or laws by which a self-interested party must operate, can help align self-interests. Transparency and fact-checking can give people more accurate information on which to base their decisions, making them less susceptible to the self-interest of others.

By way of example, consider a generic political race. Ideally, we want to make sure that it's one man, one vote so that no one can unduly influence the outcome. We don't want one candidate having ten times the funds of the other candidate, fearing that the election might be "bought." And if someone is giving lots of money to one candidate, we'd want to know who he or she is, and what he or she stands for.[143] Further, if the candidates stated facts or quoted statistics, we'd want to know if they were true, false or a matter of opinion. Having fair and just rules, transparency and accountability all put limits on rampant self-interest.

---

[143] [A] ...recent Times-CBS poll found that an extraordinary 92 percent of Americans want full disclosure of campaign contributors - far many more than, say, believe in evolution. But they will not get their wish anytime soon." Rich, Frank. "Still the Best Congress Money Can Buy." New York Times, November 27, 2010.

CHAPTER 18: THE ALIGNMENT OF SELF-INTERESTS

What happens when self-interests clash? Taking a two-person situation, what happens when each likes and wants to do different activities, or hold very different beliefs?

Let's start with two friends, John and Robert, who have known each other since high school. They are both athletes and enjoy running together, and occasionally play tennis, although their legs complain more loudly each year. Robert likes to go to movies and John would rather watch sports on TV. What happens if and when they disagree? Not much. They do play tennis and go running together, but Robert goes to the movies with other friends or his wife, and John stays home and watches his favorite teams on TV. Not a problem. Let's also say that Robert is liberal , and John is conservative. Still no problem. They can play a few sets of tennis and maybe even go out for a beer afterwards, but avoid talking about politics. Or, maybe argue a little (or razz each other) over politics while drinking their beer, go home and see each other next month. It's not important that one convince the other. The point is that friendships can easily handle differences between people. John knows that he can't, won't and has no right to change Robert and vice versa. Live and let live. No one wins, no one loses. They can focus their friendship on similarities, enjoying the things they both like to do, talk about things they have in common, such as old times and old friends, and ignore all their differences.

Looking at the friendship, we say that John and Robert's ISIs are *aligned* for tennis, jogging and the memories they share, and not much else. On the other hand, it doesn't seem to matter. Both John and Robert satisfy areas in which their ISIs are *not* aligned with other people. Robert goes to the movies with his wife and John watches Monday Night football with other male friends.

Our friends change over time, meaning that at various times in our lives, our interests align with different people. We may grow apart from some, grow closer to others, depending on what fills our ISIs at a particular point in our lives.

What happens in marriage, where you can't put alignment of interests on the shelf for a month or so? We know that spouses can't be clones of one another and therefore have different ISIs by degrees. The *more* the ISIs of the couple diverges, that is, the *less* aligned their self-interests, the more potential there is for strife. Consider a marriage in which the woman is quite social and the man is not. He finds parties and get-togethers unrewarding and unpleasant. She thrives on them. He enjoys watching TV and playing video games, and she has no interest in either.

Unless something changes, either the wife will be unhappy (if they don't often go out socially) or the husband will (if they do go out often). A rule might be... *If one person wins consistently, they both lose.* If they do go out, the husband pouts, and his wife will pay a price later. If they stay home, she is bored to tears, and he will know of her displeasure. As stated above, the greater the differences the more potential for strife.

A lack of alignment of self-interests can be dealt with by compromise. Four methods of compromise were offered in a previous chapter which involved Averaging, Veto Power, Alternation of Realms, or Alternation of Choices Within Realms. For example, the couple above might agree to go out socially once a week, which is less than she would like but more than he would choose. Or, if they go out, he could veto certain situations that make him uncomfortable, such as parties where he knows no one, and that she could veto some TV shows that she finds odious.

If compromise is sought by both husband and wife, they may prevent their differences from growing and provide a paradigm for resolving new differences as they arise over time. If one or both members of the pair aren't willing to compromise, the pair may grow further apart. That is, their self-interests become less and less aligned.

Marriage counseling may simply be defined as helping a couple to realign, or better align their self-interests. And if these interests can't be aligned, either by the couple alone or with the help of a therapist, the couple may split up. If one partner's needs for intimacy and affection aren't met, and the other partner, both on his own and in counseling fails to compromise or change, the relationship may end, or result in infidelity.

Other situations, such as a parent-teen relationship follow similar patterns. If a teen gets no pleasure from school for any of a variety of reasons (lack of interest in the subjects, inability to comprehend the material or to pay attention) his attention will drift in class, he'll miss homework assignments and may cut school. This goes directly against the SI of his parents and eventually against his own SI (so that his SI is misguided). A way has to be found to align the self-interests of the teen and his parents. Possible solutions include getting the teen into easier classes with "cooler" teachers, getting him more help and support, counseling or medication if depression or A.D.D. is a factor, or rewards or consequences at home. All of these factors are discussed in "Parents and Teens: a Guide to Peaceful Coexistence" by the this author.[144]

To generalize, any differences between and among people can be seen as a non-alignment of self-interests. The same seems to hold whether we are talking about two individuals, groups of people, or nations. The job of a politician running for office is to align her self-interest with that of the people she wants to serve. The one whose SI is most closely aligned with the voting public will likely win

[144] Outskirts Press, 2008.

election. The controversial health care reform bill of 2009 provides another example. Each person, given different information of widely varying accuracy, tries to assess if the reform packages fits their needs. Will it cover what they need covered now and in the future, and will it increase or decrease their cost? If they think it serves them, they will be for the bill. If not, they'll oppose it. If they think that what is in the bill aligns with their self-interest, they will be for it.

There are three conceptual schemes, all borrowed from mathematics, that can help us visualize and understand, alignment of self-interests. The first two will be discussed in this chapter, the third will be explained in detail in the next.

The first rubric involves Venn diagrams. Look below:

Couple that has much in common:

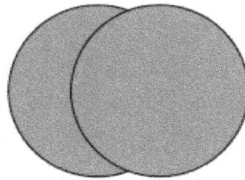

Couple that has many things in common:

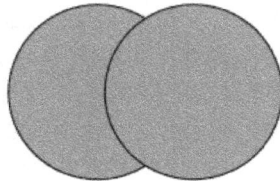

Couple that has very little in common:

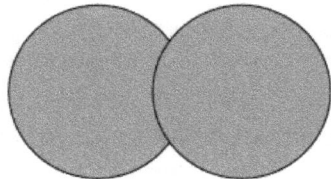

In each of the three pairs of circles, the self-interest of each spouse, or person in a dyad, is represented by the area covered by the circle.   In the top diagram, the two circles overlap a great deal. That is, the area that they both share is relatively large in relation to the area that they do not share. In effect, much of their self-interest is aligned.

The middle set of circles reflects less alignment of ISIs and the bottom set shows still less. The idea of compromise and/or counseling is to make the circles overlap to a greater extent, so that the circles, and the ISIs become more aligned.

A second way of looking at alignment, non-alignment, and everything in between is through the concept of vectors borrowed from math and physics. A vector is a mathematical quantity that has both a magnitude and direction. If I say I am walking a mile, that represents magnitude. If I say that I am walking one mile east, that gives both magnitude and direction. Vectors are usually represented by one-way arrows, the magnitude being in proportion to the length of the arrow.

Vectors are manipulable mathematically. If the interests of two people are aligned, the arrows are pointing in the same direction, and their magnitudes add.
So that...

An example of this is if two friends both vote for the same candidate in an election. Their self-interests are totally in alignment and their votes add together.

If the interests of the two people are totally *unaligned*, as in if one friend votes for one candidate and the other friend votes for the other, their votes cancel each other out. It's the same as adding a number and the negative of that number:

There are situations where the self-interest of two people falls somewhere between total alignment and total nonalignment. Clark wants to eat out but prefers Chinese food. His wife, Marge also wants to eat out, but prefers Mexican. If they can compromise, either by flipping a coin, alternating choices, or picking a third type of cuisine, say Thai, the vector representation might look like:

Clark/Chinese   compromise/Thai

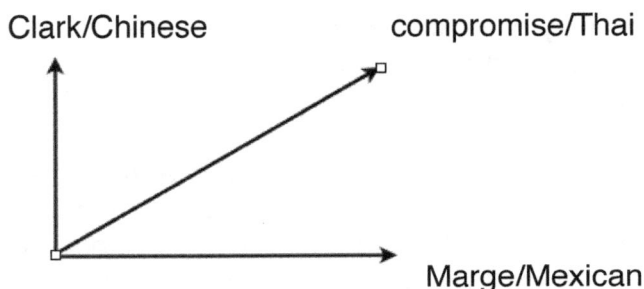

                                 Marge/Mexican

Note that Marge's vector is longer than Clark's because she cares more about the decision than he does. The third vector, labeled "compromise/Thai," is the result of adding, or resolving, Clark's and Marge's vectors which represent their ISIs.

The Venn diagrams and vector analyses are not important in and of themselves. They are tools that may be used to conceptualize, understand and, perhaps, quantify the self-interests of individuals, groups and nations. A third tool, that of correlation, will be employed in the next chapter to discuss Collective Self-Interest.

CHAPTER 19: COLLECTIVE SELF-INTEREST

Arnold the Author, a financial planner, writes a book entitled "Getting Rich by Investing in Asparagus." Why did Arnold write this book? Some possible reasons are:

1) He wants to make money from the sale of the book.
2) He wants to drive business to his main source of income; i.e. if he is a financial planner it may increase the number of people who want to use his services.
3) He wants to help people, which makes him feel virtuous and better about himself.
4) He wants to feel like he has accomplished something in life, i.e. he always wanted to write a book and this lets him attain that goal.
5) He wants to achieve status among his peers or family, or to generally impress people.
6) He wants to leave a legacy. The book is a piece of him that will live on after he dies.

What all of these reasons have in common (and we're sure the reader can think of others) is that they all serve Arnold's individual self-interest (ISI). Arnold may make more money, feel better about himself, scratch one item off his "bucket list," or attain greater status in the groups in which he travels. Note that all of these reasons can and may very well exist concurrently in Arnold's mind, in varying degrees at various times. Arnold may write his book mainly to make money and enjoy the attention accorded a minor vegetable celebrity. Amy may write a book because she's always wanted to do that, and consider the money she makes as much less relevant.

Individual self-interest, I believe, is the primary motivation for all behavior. If we want to consider the interface between the individual and larger society, ISI must be taken into account when considering ecological, social or political issues otherwise we're missing the boat. If gas prices go up, people are motivated to "go green" by driving less, but mostly because they are saving a buck. We recognize that a small cohort may drive less without financial incentive, their ISIs being fed by feeling virtuous (or less guilty, superior to others, or politically correct). Going green alone may be desirable to most, but not enough to get them to change their behaviors unless and until their pocketbooks are affected. Saving money provides the "tipping point" in their decisions.

In order to consider broader issues, we need to define another term. We've already defined what we've called "Individual Self-Interest," or ISI. Basically, ISI is served by anything that makes us feel good or helps us to avoid feeling bad as an individual. Making money, loving our children, being proud of ourselves, feeling that we have accomplished something, feeling that we have helped someone, feeling safer or more secure, in addition to more primitive activities such as eating and having sex, all make us feel good. Reducing anxiety or uncertainty, letting go of anger, shedding guilt and getting out of a funk, all make us feel less bad, and thus serve ISI.

What if we'd like to consider our planet and its living inhabitants? Let us define "Collective Self-Interest," or CSI. Behaviors that help sustain all the living organisms on the planet serve CSI. Behaviors that support plants and animals, humans among them, serve CSI. Our belief is that people are entitled to have enough to eat, have clean water to drink, have a roof over their head, and have access to medical treatment. Most of the tenets found in the good books of all religions (e.g. the Ten Commandments) offer guidelines for promoting CSI. Killing, raping and pillaging are all unethical actions and are antithetical to the CSI. It is hoped that the majority of humanity can agree with the "cluster" of principles that make up the CSI.

Let's now turn to the relationship between the ISI and the CSI by going back to our buddy Arnold the Author. Suppose Arnold sells three books in total. Does that help Arnold's ISI? Absolutely. Even if he makes no money from it, he will feel some degree of pride and a sense of accomplishment from its completion and publication. Not as good perhaps as making a lot of money from the book, but some good feeling nonetheless. The CSI, the good of humanity, is left unscathed however. Three books are not likely to help many people (except, of course, Arnold's mother, who is very, very proud).

But what if Arnold sells a million of his pithy tomes? Certainly his ISI is served well. In addition to the pride and sense of accomplishment there is significant financial gain. Well done, Arnie! Is the CSI served? Yes, by degrees, largely depending on the subject matter of the book. If Arnold's title is a romantic novel or a taut thriller ("The Da Vinci Code" comes to mind) many people will get enjoyment, perhaps slightly affecting the CSI. Or if the subject matter is an innovative diet plan that makes many people healthier or an inspirational treatise that leads people to change their behavior for the good (e.g. stop smoking, go green, go on a healthy asparagus diet) the effect on the CSI will be strong and positive. Now for another digression...

Many of us know the statistical concept of correlation. If we say that two variables (or measures) are highly correlated, we mean that when one goes up, the other goes up, or when one goes down the other goes down. For example, the higher a person's income, the more likely it will be that they own a big home. There is a strong *positive* relationship between income and size of home. This is not true all the time, but *most* of the time. If it were true *all* of the time, we would say that the correlation coefficient (the measure of the strength of the relationship) equals +1.00.

If, on the other hand, whenever one measure goes up, the other goes down, we say that there is a strong *negative* correlation. An example of this would be that the more education a person has, the less likely they are to be poor. As education goes up, poverty goes down. Not a perfect correlation, but a strong one. A perfect negative correlation would be -1.00.

Sometimes two variables bear no relationship to one another. We say there is no correlation between them (or that the correlation coefficient is 0.00). Height and income probably have close to a zero correlation. Some tall people make a lot of money, some make much less.[145]

The correlation coefficient thus runs from -1.00 (perfect negative relationship) through 0.00 (no relationship) to +1.00 (perfect positive relationship). In reality, we rarely get perfect correlation, but correlation by degrees. Height and weight have an intermediate positive correlation of approximately +.70.[146] If you are tall, you are likely to weigh more than if you are short. Age and health have a moderate negative

---

[145] Believe it or not, this has been studied: Judge, T. A., & Cable, D. M. (2004). "The effect of physical height on workplace success and income: Preliminary test of a theoretical model." Journal of Applied Psychology, 89, 428-441, 2004. There are also studies that indicate a strong correlation between nutrition and height.

[146] http://www.webster.edu/~woolflm/correlation/correlation.html.

correlation.[147] If you are older, you are less likely to be healthy than if you are younger.

Now we'll return to our conversation about Collective Self-Interest and Individual Self-Interest. We believe, and we believe that almost everyone believes, that the more we work towards Collective Self-Interest, the better. The more we are ethical, the more people we prevent from going hungry, the more we keep our planet inhabitable the better.[148]   But what about ISI?

ISI is always there. We're always looking out for number one. But there are some pursuits of self-interest that *promote* CSI, some that bear no relationship to CSI and some that actually work *against* CSI. In other words, we need to examine the correlation between ISI and CSI. Some examples:

STRONG POSITIVE CORRELATION between ISI and
     CSI:

> I teach someone to farm. I feel good about myself for helping someone (serving my Individual Self-Interest) while the person who I teach can now feed herself better and pass on the knowledge to others (serving the Collective Self-Interest).

---

[147] http://ideas.repec.org/p/mcm/sedapp/57.html.

[148] It may also be useful to consider groups of intermediate size. For example, how does the CSI of all the residents of California correlate with the CSI of the residents of Ohio (it may depend on the issue)? Or how does the CSI of one nation correlate with the CSI of its neighbor, or its ally or adversary? Perhaps, if CSI is reserved for all of humanity, that this concept would be better served by a different term, such as "Group Self-Interest," or GSI.

I teach someone to read. I feel good (ISI),
earn a living (ISI) and help others (CSI).

I take my bike to work instead of my car, or I
replace my light bulbs with energy-efficient
ones, I recycle. I save money, improve my
health and feel virtuous (ISI) while helping the
planet (CSI).

LOW OR NEAR-ZERO CORRELATION between ISI
and CSI:

I build myself a shed which makes me feel
like I've accomplished something (ISI) but
I've used a small amount of the Earth's
resources up, so my project has a *slight*
negative effect on CSI.

I collect stamps, or read a book, or listen to
music because I enjoy them (ISI) having
virtually no effect on the world one way or the
other (CSI).

STRONG NEGATIVE CORRELATION between ISI and CSI:

I rob houses in a neighborhood to get money to buy
drugs. This serves my (misguided) ISI, while at
the same time hurting those that I've victimized and
creating an aura of fear in that area. I've adversely
affected the CSI for my own gain.

I have a lot of money and buy a big SUV and larger
home than I need, both of which make me happy
(ISI). I use up more than my share of the Earth's
resources, thus in a small way both driving up the
price for others and contributing to global warming.
This reduces CSI.

These correlations provide a way to put a value on our actions. We need to look for behaviors where the self-interest of the individual promotes the self-interest of the people of the world. In other words, where ISI and CSI have as high a positive correlation as possible. Conversely, we need to avoid or work against situations in which the correlation between individual and collective self-interest is negative.

Even if the correlation between ISI and CSI is high, we need to be modest in our expectations. David Brooks points out, in effect, the difference between exerting effort and controlling the whole situation. He makes a distinction between "...discrete good and systemic good. ...When you are the president in a financial crisis, you have the power to pave roads and hire teachers. That will reduce the suffering of real people who would otherwise be jobless. You have the power to streamline regulations and reduce tax burdens. That will induce a bit more hiring and activity. These are real contributions. But you don't have the power to transform the whole situation. Your discrete goods might contribute to an overall turnaround, but that turnaround will be beyond your comprehension and control."[149]

Correlations between ISI and CSI may change over time. In the summer of 2008. with gas at four dollars per gallon, most people cut down on the miles they drove, saving them money and benefitting the CSI at the same time. By December of 2008, the price of gas dropped below two dollars per gallon. Now more people could afford to drive to see people or do things that they enjoyed, raising their ISI, but at the cost of lowering CSI (more miles driven, more CO_2 released, more dependence on foreign oil, more global warming, etc.). And, obviously, there may be situations where the national self-interest of one nation

---

[149] Brooks, David. "The Planning Fallacy." New York Times Op-Ed, September 15, 2011.

(e.g. a petroleum exporter) may come into conflict with that of another (a petroleum importer).

An interesting example can be found on a different playing field, that of a typical high school. Kids get a feeling of accomplishment from a variety of sources in their teen years. Some feel good for being good athletes. Others get pleasure from the social life that high school affords. Some strive for popularity. Some want to have the fastest, coolest car. Other teens are into drugs or alcohol, and strive to be the ones that provide the illegal substances or use the most of them. Some teens isolate and feel good if they can be the best at video games that they play against others over the Internet. Others are studious and feel good when they get good grades. Note that any or all of these actions by teens is feeding their ISI.

We would argue that the studious types represent a high correlation between ISI and CSI (they feel good when they do well and have a good chance of making contributions to society later on). The kids who drink and use drugs have the best chance of being a drain on society in adulthood (rehabs, prison, inability to hold a job, dropping out of school) and thus the ISI and CSI have a potentially large negative correlation.

Other groups fall in between. Teens for whom social life is important may grow up to value their communities and serve them. "Gearheads" may grow up to be great car mechanics and take their rightful place in society. Athletes may grow up to be coaches for their own and others' children. In these cases, the correlation between ISI and CSI may also be positive.

A second example relates to the choices for presidential Cabinet positions. By leaning towards the best and brightest, people with experience but who can think flexibly, the President has the best chance of getting people who will fulfill his/her ISI and the appointees' ISI as they work together for the collective self-interest. Some electees choose those whose main qualification is that they are loyal, thus serving their own ISI through nepotism, but this often works against the CSI. The manner in which a President comports him or herself can also be positive or negative for CSI.

Battle cries such as "Drill, Baby, Drill," "Mission Accomplished" or "America: Love it or leave it!" are simplistic and often work against the CSI. These statements may temporarily make some in the United States feel proud of our country, in a slight way working to serve the ISIs of the population. A collateral result, however, is to lower the opinion of the American government in the eyes of many of the more than 6 billion inhabitants of the world and their respective governments. When nations are at odds with each other, this spills over into areas where cooperation is needed. The less cooperation between nations, the less the CSI is served.

Let's be grandiose. Suppose we are trying to decide which of human actions are good, which are bad, and which are neither. Let us define actions that either (a) increase the life expectancy of any or all humans by any amount of time or (b) improve the quality of life for any or all humans as good. We will assume that these actions *benefit* the Collective Self-Interest.

Many of these actions are scalable and can happen *by degrees*. A program that provides clean drinking water for a thousand people is better than one that provides clean water for ten people. A program that provides drinkable water for those who have none is better than a program that provides improved drinking water for those who already have access to drinkable water. A drug that cures a fatal disease afflicting a million people is better than one that cures a thousand. Providing solar panels for those who have no access to electricity is better than providing solar panels for those who already have access to the electrical grid.

Every action occurs within one or more systems. That is, everything affects everything else, also by degrees. If someone smokes a cigar in Topeka, it affects, in small measure, everyone else on the planet. If I spend $10 at

Walmart, I am affecting the United States economy in a minor way, depending on how much of the product is produced domestically, which affects all the other economies in the world. Theoretically, because actions take place in systems, the actions can have both positive and negative effects on CSI. A coal plant in China can have negative effects on the rest of the world, yet have positive effects on the local economy and the well-being of Chinese people in general.

Individual Self-Interest is instinctual and biological and is, a priori, neutral to CSI. ISI can, however, be shaped or directed to either work for, against, or be neutral to the CSI. In other words, an individual can do things that help, harm or are neutral to people in particular or humanity in general. A noble task would be to promote ISI actions that correlate positively with CSI, so that humans act not only in their own self-interest but in the interest of the greater good at the same time.

Some things that are happening today are inevitable, meaning we have little or no control over them. They include globalization of trade, increased interconnectedness of people, increased interdependence among nations, inexorably advancing technology, shifts in global consumption, utilization of resources, and power, increased availability of information and specialization of knowledge. Even though they are largely inevitable, the actions are affected by human control, and thus they can be neutral, positive or negative to CSI.

If we were trying to cull a sort of "Ten Principles of Collective Self-Interest" we might take beliefs from the canons of all the major religions, as well as the U.S. Constitution and combine them into a "cluster of constructs" that benefit the CSI. A list of them might look something like this: [150]

---

[150] Adapted from an unpublished manuscript, "Future Common Sense: Adapting to a Green, Global and Egalitarian Planet." By Gribin, Anthony J. and Drossman, Howard.

TEN PRINCIPLES OF COLLECTIVE SELF-INTEREST

1) Increase the Sustainability of the Planet for Living Organisms. Whether or not God created it, Earth is still the only game in town, at least for now. We should keep it habitable for as many species as possible, including us.

2) Increase Biodiversity. The more biodiverse the planet, the better it is for other species and the greater resilience there is to losses in ecosystem function.

3) Reduce or Slow Global Warming. Our best minds tell us that we are in possible danger or rapid changes in climate over short periods of time which will adversely affect millions if not billions of people. Even if we were not, the following corollaries make economic sense:

   Reduce our carbon footprints
   Sequester CO_2
   Reduce emissions of greenhouse gases

4) Extend Life Expectancies for the World's Poor. Work towards curing diseases.
   Research into curing disease and developing better health practices.
   Teach prevention and proper health routines.
   Work towards Universal Health Care.

5) Promote a Better Quality of Life.
   Reduce Suffering.
   Reduce Poverty and Income Inequality.
   Promote Education.
   Make necessary resources available to all (clean water, food, shelter).

Reduce crime against people and property.

6) Consume Less and Live More Moderately.
Increase efficiency through technology.
Build appropriate transportation and living spaces.
Travel and drive less, telecommute to work.
Buy and eat local when possible.
Reduce energy use.

7) Promote equality.
Increase Egalitarianism. We should not need to look down on other people. "Do Unto Other As You Would Have Them Do Unto You" (Golden Rule).
Decrease Sectarianism. Less division should result in less bias and prejudice, and war.
Promote humility and decrease swagger.

8) Promote Truth, Accountability and Responsibility.
Reduce bias.
Increase responsible use of the Internet while keeping it free of commercial control.
Increase accountability for computer and cell phone use.
Reduce obfuscation in media (political ads).

9) Reduce Uncertainty.
Precautionary Principle. If we are wrong about Global Warming, no big deal. If we are right, and do nothing to stem the tide, we're in big trouble.
Regulate corporations for environmental and labor practices.
Allow investment only in real capital.
Amend our laws (Constitution) to adapt to change.

10) Teach CSI-friendly Values To Our Children

Promote greater understanding of ourselves and
others.
Promote flexibility, so that humans can adapt to a
changing future.
Promote compromise and search for win-win
solutions to problems.
Promote effortful behavior, not results-oriented
behavior.
Promote an understanding of ecology, systems,
culture and science.

Okay, now that we have an idea of the things that
comprise and promote the Collective Self-Interest, what
now? Well...notice anything about the goals listed above?
We think that they are relatively *unchanging*. Increasing
sustainability and biodiversity will *always* be good.
Extending life expectancies for the world's poor, improving
quality of life, promoting equality and reducing bias will
always be good. Saving one life in sub-Saharan Africa will
be the same as saving one life in southeast Asia. Saving
two lives in Darfur will be better than saving one life in
Darfur. So, if we want to change things for the better, to
increase CSI, our only option is to work on, or manipulate,
ISI.

For example, taking liberty with reality, suppose
North Fleebonia is a poor country that happens to be the
home of the extremely cute North Fleebonian tree frog.
What would happen if said tree frog were to become all the
rage among global pre-teens. Our guess is that the
economy of North Fleebonia might improve, leading to
cleaner drinking water, more food and less disease among
native Fleebonians.

Or using the Olympic model, suppose that one
nation, Bonzo, was designated "Country of the Year" by the
United Nations. Along with this designation would come
advertising campaigns and television coverage of the
culture, places of interest and travel within Bonzo. We

might expect, again, that people that like to travel might start booking trips to and tours of Bonzo and that the prosperity of Bonzonites might concurrently improve.

Another model for linking ISI and CSI is provided by spirituality and/or religion. If we believe that a molecule of water is our bodies is the same as a molecule of water in a turnip, that implies that we are all a part of the natural world and have an obligation to care for mother earth and promote CSI. Planting trees may make us feel better and help humanity at the same time. If our religious teachings direct us to help others, which makes us feel less guilty, it also serves to promote the CSI.

Or how about using the "Oscar" model. Suppose some world organization, such as the Nobel Committee, decides to recognize second tier world leaders. Let's face it, the Nobel Peace prize is great, but how many of us are in that league? There aren't that many Al Gores running around. Suppose we gave out several awards, let's call them "Worldies," for "Best Up-and-Coming World Leader," or "Leader Who Improved Health Care the Most" in any given year. The idea is to create status for citizens of the world to aspire to, thus feeding their own ISI while supporting CSI. Perhaps we can create a competition to see who can be next year's "Most Benevolent Despot."

And although these examples are facetious (though "Dancing With the Dictators" does have a certain ring to it), they do point the way. We can manipulate the ISI by fiat (consequences for drunk driving), through creating economic incentives (manipulating the price of fuel), or by teaching values to our children. If we teach values such as the ones enumerated above in the Ten Principles, we will "grow" adults who seek to fulfill their own ISI by increasing CSI. They will feel better if they can reduce poverty, or seek a career that might eventually find a cure for a disease, or even live more moderately so as to use up less of the Earth's resources. They too, will be increasing their own ISI.

Chapter 20: Lessons Learned

At the beginning of this book, a gauntlet was laid down. We decided to test the hypothesis that humans act in their own self-interest all of the time, in every arena. To do this, we assumed its truth, and sought to explain seemingly contrary behaviors such as altruism, patriotism, charity, delay of gratification, self-defeating behaviors as well as the ordinary actions involved in living day to day. Did the theory hold water? Did it account for some of the observed facts, most of them or all of them. By now, the reader can predict our conclusion.

The most mundane of behaviors are easily explained by Selfonomics. Greed, political choice and decision making all fall easily into the swath cut by broadly defined self-interest. Altruism falls prey as well, as long as seeing another person's smile is rewarding to us, or makes us feel less bad about our own good fortune.

Religion fits the model also. We are not saying that there is no God, but the theory of self-interest, all the time, must account for the possibility that God does not exist as well as for his or her existence. It does both well.

The examples provided in this book are far from exhaustive, are surely biased and are presented with a less than rigorous scientific approach. But if 99.9% of the data *seems* to fit a curve, any theory that gave birth to that curve needs to be taken very very seriously. Look, even the number we use for pi is an approximation.

It would seem that a theory, based on ordinary behavior, that seems to explain everything, would have surfaced before. Maybe the answers were too close to us, too much a part of us, for them to be noticeable. Paul Krugman, op-Ed columnist for the New York Times and Nobel Laureate in Economics, recently wrote a column summing up the economy of the decade between 2000 and

2009.[151] "So here's what... just about everyone in a policy-making position at the time, believed in 1999: America has honest corporate accounting; this lets investors make good decisions, and also forces management to behave responsibly; and the result is a stable, well-functioning financial system. What percentage of all this turned out to be true? Zero. ...What was truly impressive about the decade past, however, was our unwillingness, as a nation, to learn from our *mistakes*." (Italics ours.)

From the viewpoint of Selfonomics, these "mistakes" are not mistakes at all. The only error is to *consider* them as mistakes. They are the accumulated natural, predictable and inevitable consequences of people following what God, biology or social learning leads them to do: look out for their own self-interest. We have to learn that people will not change. We can only hope to define parameters that will *channel* self-interest in appropriate directions.

Ben Bernanke, Chairman of the Federal Reserve, said the same thing that we've said, in a different way. "Stronger regulation and supervision aimed at problems with underwriting practices and lenders' risk management would have been a more effective and surgical approach to constraining the housing bubble than a general increase in interest rates."[152] If the rules were stronger governing interest-only loans, there wouldn't have been so many foreclosures and the collapse in the housing market would've been less serious. In other words, don't expect people to change. Change the rules by which they must behave. "A system of compensation that provides huge bonuses based on short-term profits necessarily ignores the long-term interests of investors. As does a system that ignores the creditworthiness of borrowers; allows credit

---

[151] Krugman, Paul. "The Big Zero." New York Times Op-Ed, December 27, 2009.

[152] Rampell, Catherine. "Lax Oversight Caused Crisis, Bernanke Says." New York Times, January 4, 2009.

rating agencies to be paid by those they rate and encourages the creation of highly complex and deceptive financial instruments. In each case, the actions - and profits - of the financial agents became insulated from both the interests of investors and the wealth-creating needs of industry."[153]

The thought of "channeling" self-interest led me to an analogy involving rivers. The study of the flow of rivers or watercourses is called fluviology. I don't know much about rivers, but it is clear that unless the source of the flow is stopped, the water is just going to keep coming downhill in a predetermined path. Imagine a stream flowing down a mountain over rocks. The water will cover the rocks, filling in gaps between them in more or less the same direction until either erosion of the rocks or the silt in the stream bed itself allows a change of course, or until an obstacle appears (e.g. a rock rolls into the stream from a higher source) somewhere in the path so that the water is forced to change course.

The stream bed is akin to the nexus of parameters; that is, rules, laws and customs, within which humans operate. The rules allow certain expressions of self-interest and deny others. Sometimes the rocks erode, allowing water to flow in a slightly different direction; sometimes rules can be bent resulting in self-interest running amok through financial swindles, cheating on a spouse, or theft through the internet.

The best, and in fact, the only way to modify the direction that self-interest takes, is to change the rules. In effect build a dam, a levee, a canal to change the flow of self-interest by changing the rules that self-interest must abide (ignoring illegality). And if we don't change the rules, and expect people to just wake up and not be driven to look out for themselves, aren't we going to run into a wall? As a matter of fact, isn't repeating the same behavior and

---

[153] Bernstein, J.M. "Hegel on Wall Street." New York Times, Op-Ed, October 3, 2010.

expecting different results a pop-sarcastic definition of insanity?

Examples of these kind of rule changes are rife on these pages, but for review, here are a few examples, some specific, others general:

1) Pass stricter clean-air, and/or carbon emission legislation. The most effective venue for this is surely an international body.   Individual Americans or Chinese cannot and should not be counted on to stop polluting unless there is incentive, legal, financial or otherwise, for them to do so. In order to affect individual Americans or Chinese, each government must see it is in the self-interest of its citizens to pass legislation to reduce pollution. And each government is more likely to do this is there is an international agreement. Self-interests will then be traded.

2) Make financial institutions and practices more transparent. The more open the financial industry, the harder it will be to skirt the laws or even work within the laws in societally unacceptable ways. Shareholders are less likely to put up with huge Wall Street perks in down times, but they first have to know about them. Dodd-Frank, which was signed into law in 2010, is a step in the right direction.

3) Give incentives for people to do what is good for the community, the country or the planet. Tax credits for clean energy and financial disincentives for owning a gas guzzler come to mind. As do grants or tax incentives to train medical personnel, including physicians, physician's assistants, nurse practitioners and nurses.

4) Don't blame the people who are most successful at their jobs. In an op-Ed piece for the New York Times, Maureen Dowd, in her inimitable way, skewered the head of Goldman Sachs and the whole issue of seemingly unsupportable bonus packages. "Goldmine Sachs, as it's

known, is out for Goldmine Sachs."[154] Not fair, in my opinion. GS played by the rules and won. If you don't like it, don't expect people to stop looking out for themselves; change the rules. And the same Constitution that allows Dowd to make mince meat, rightly or wrongly, out of the person or the company of her choice, is the same country that allows GS to just be GS.

In the same vein, instead of complaining that ball players make too much money and that some teams literally buy championships, equalize things by mandating that each team spend the same amount on its workforce (or at least limit the range of differences) if they want to belong to the exclusive club that is Major League Baseball. A given team could sign a few expensive players and fill in with cheaper, less experienced players, or they could spread the money around more. Fantasy baseball leagues often adopt this approach. The result would be that teams in Kansas City, Seattle and Cincinnati can compete on equal footing with those in New York, Boston and L.A. And yes, there would be unintended consequences to this scheme, some negative, but also some positive.

5) If technology puts too much power in the hands of too few, change the rules by changing ways that information can flow over the internet, or by licensing information providers and holding them to standards that are more geared to the masses than the needs of the few. As with financial practices and transactions, make internet use more transparent. Freedom of speech is essential, but with it should come the responsibility to own up to what has been said. I should be able to say whatever I want to say, but why shouldn't I be held responsible for any harm caused by my words?

---

[154] Dowd, Maureen. "Virtuous Bankers? Really!?!" New York Times, Op-Ed, November 11, 2009.

6) So the next generation can learn from our mistakes, research into ISI, DSI, PSI, MSI, and the ratios among them, for individuals, groups and even countries, would make us wiser. In therapy, looking at the ratio of a patient's PSI to DSI or MSI to DSI would be instructive for both the therapist and patient. Patterns of DSI and PSI over the average person's life cycle would be interesting, as would correlations between a person's ISI and societal CSI.

7) Teaching critical thinking (as well as self-interest theory and logic) early in school may make children into more discerning consumers of information as adults. Talking about self-interest, though perhaps initially creating more cynicism, will lead to better discernment, fairer practices and more informed decisions.

8) A new profession of "Self-Interest Predictor," with the task of predicting how self-interest might run amok, would be worth developing. Computer software makers hire hackers to try and break their codes so they can develop defenses against these intrusions. Military strategists game various geopolitical situations to be ready for any contingency and scientists use computer modeling to try and predict natural disasters. The Self-Interest Predictor would be charged with trying to find flaws in the laws and rules in the financial and political systems to predict how self-interested parties will try to skirt the rules and or benefit at the expense of others.

     The job of this person would to recommend re-channeling the "rivers" of self-interest (ISI) in ways that are in tighter accord with the needs of the human race (CSI). I picture the requirements as including, but not limited to, a strong knowledge of ethics, mathematics, law, economics and psychology. The person would be a consultant, a problem solver and an information provider at all levels of society, from the family, to the community, to the government. They may eventually be seen as our "wise elders," who keep us on the straight and narrow. As the

Federal Reserve does with interest rates, our SIPs would help us balance the needs of our people by recommending patches to the existing systems of rules and laws that channel our individual and collective self-interests. It's kind of like have an Army Corps of Engineers to protect us from what our own self-interest has wrought.

9) Finally, another profession, that of "Fact Checker," would help to ensure that we minimize the inaccuracy of the information that is being thrown at us. Today, well-respected newspapers establish criteria for fact-checking before they go to print with a story, the F.D.A. filters our drug choices to ensure safety, rating agencies clear movies for children and bond rating agencies provide information about the safety of our investments. Information is already being vetted in small measure. Snopes.com reports on the truth or falsity of "urban legends." Wikipedia, the online encyclopedia, lets the public correct misinformation.

Having an agency comprised of fact checkers or bias assessors would help people come to more accurate judgments in a world that bombards us with a myriad of opinions. Impartiality and reliance on scientific evidence would be part of the package. Newsmakers may still have political or self-serving agendas, but at least we would be more aware of them. The right of free speech would be untouched, but at least we'd know if what we're hearing is true, false or just a matter of opinion. As was recently pointed out about a candidate running for the nomination in the 2012 Presidential race, "Everyone is entitled to his or her own opinion. ...But he's not entitled to his own facts."[155] Perhaps all political ads and the output of the major sources of news would have to pass by such a fact checking agency. Ads, broadsides, articles and news broadcasts would carry more weight if they had some kind of a "Seal of Approval" from some such agency.

---

[155] Andersen, Kurt. "Our Politics Are Sick." New York Times Op-Ed, August 19, 2011.

Back to self-interest. We've spent most of this book finding that "self-interest will out." It is encouraged by political systems and economic activity, it guides social and romantic behavior, it protects us after spinal operations. It is always there; it is never on holiday. It is like the flow of water in a river; inexorable. And, considering that the survival of the fittest implies that those with more aggressive self-interest will outlast the rest, the "flow" of self-interest is not likely to be stemmed any time soon. We'd almost have to be re-bred, but even that wouldn't work because from the new time zero, the most self-interested would survive longer. The best we can do is recognize, talk about and correct for the abuses of expressions of self-interest.

References

Altman, Morris, ed. (2006). <u>Handbook of Contemporary Behavioral Economics: Foundations and Developments.</u> Armonk, N.Y.: M.E. Sharpe, Inc.

Andersen, Kurt. "Our Politics Are Sick." New York Times Op-Ed, August 19, 2011.

Andreoni, James. "Impure Altruism and Donations to Public Goods: A Theory of Warm-Glow Giving?" The Economic Journal, 1990, p. 464-77.

Ariely, D. (2008). <u>Predictably Irrational.</u> HarperCollins.

Bernstein, J.M. "Hegel on Wall Street." New York Times Op-Ed, October 3, 2010.

Blow, Charles. "A Nation of Cowards?" New York Times Op-Ed, February 20, 2009.

Blow, Charles "A Profile of Online Profiles," New York Times Op-Ed, September 9, 2009.

Blow, Charles. "Them That's Not Shall Lose." New York Times Op-Ed, June 24, 2011.

Bonabeau, Eric, Dorigo, Marco & Theraulaz, Guy. "Swarm Intelligence: From Natural to Artificial Studies," New York: Oxford University Press, 1999. Proceedings of the Santa Fe Institute Studies in the Sciences of Complexity.

Brooks, David. "In Search of Dignity." New York Times Op-Ed, July 7, 2009.

Brooks, David. "Missing Dean Acheson," New York Times Op-Ed, August 1, 2008.

Brooks, David. "Pundit Under Protest." New York Times, Op-Ed, June 14, 2011.

Brooks, David. "The Unexamined Society." New York Times Op-Ed, July 7, 2011.

Brooks, David. "The Grand Bargain Lives!" New York Times Op-Ed, July 21, 2011.

Brooks, David. "The Vigorous Virtues." New York Times Op-Ed September 1, 2011.

Brooks, David. "The Planning Fallacy." New York Times Op-Ed, September 15, 2011.

Bruni, Frank. "Humble Service With a Side of Swag." New York Times Op-Ed, August 20, 2011.

Bueno de Mesquita, Bruno. (2009). The Predictioneer's Game: Using the Logic of Brazen Self-Interest to See and Shape the Future. Random House, New York.

Cohan, William D. "The Power of Failure." New York Times Opinionator, November 26, 2010.

Collins, Gail. "A Right to Bear Glocks?" New York Times Op-Ed, January 9, 2011.

Dawkins, R. (2006). The Selfish Gene (30th Anniversary Edition). New York City: Oxford University Press.

De Young, Raymond. "Expanding and Evaluating Motives for Environmentally Responsible Behavior." Journal of Social Issues, Vol. 56, No. 3, 2000, pp. 509-526.

Douthat, Ross. "The Devil and Joe Paterno." New York Times Op-Ed November 13, 2011.

Dowd, Maureen. "Virtuous Bankers? Really!?!" New York Times Op-Ed, November 11, 2009.

Dowd, Maureen. "Eggheads and Blockheads." New York Times Op-Ed, September 18, 2011.

Egan, Timothy. "The Need for Greed." New York Times Op-Ed, May 16, 2011.

Emanuel, Dr. Zeke. Television interview: "Morning Joe," hosted by Joe Scarborough and Mika Brzesinski, on MSNBC, August 31, 2011.

Friedman, Tom. "www.jihad.com." New York Times Op-Ed, December 16, 2009.

Friedman, Thomas L. "The Whole Truth and Nothing But." New York Times Op-Ed, September 6, 2011.

Gribin, Anthony J. (2007). You're Not Nuts... You've Just Got Issues. Outskirts Press.

Gribin, Anthony J. (2008) Parents and Teens: a Guide to Peaceful Coexistence. Outskirts Press.

Gribin, Anthony J. & Drossman, Howard. Future Common Sense: Adapting to a Green, Global and Egalitarian Planet. Unpublished manuscript.

Hamermesh, Daniel S. "Ugly? You May Have A Case." New York Times, August 27, 2011.

Hayek, Friedrich August. "The Use of Knowledge in Society." The American Economic Review, 1945.

Hines, J.M., et. al. "Analysis and Synthesis of research on responsible environmental behavior: A meta-analysis." Journal of Environmental Education, 18(2), 1986/87, p. 1-8.

"How Fear Drove World Rice Markets Insane." Story broadcast on National Public Radio, November 2, 2011 on "All Things Considered." Host Robert Siegel, reported by Dan Charles.

Hume, David (1751). An Enquiry Concerning the Principles of Morals. Public domain.

Hungerford, Harold R. & Volk, Trudi L. "Changing Learner Behavior Through Environmental Education." Journal of Environmental Education, 21(3), 1990, p.8-22.

"In The Land of Denial." New York Times Editorial, September 6, 2011.

Judge, T. A., & Cable, D. M. (2004). "The effect of physical height on workplace success and income: Preliminary test of a theoretical model." Journal of Applied Psychology, 89, 428-441, 2004.

Judson, Olivia. "Back to Reality" New York Times Online, December 4, 2008.

Kaplan, Stephen. "Human Nature and Environmentally Responsible Behavior." Journal of Social Issues, Vol. 56, No. 3, 2000, pp. 491-508.

Kaswell, Alice Shirrell; Lucille Zimmerman and G. Neil Martin (2001). "It's Good to Be a YAVIS". *Improbable Research.* http:// improbable.com/airchives/paperair/volume7/v7i2/yavis-7-2 .html

King, Desmond S. & Smith, Rogers M. "On Race, the Silence Is Bipartisan." New York Times Op-Ed, September 2, 2011.

Kopeikin, Hal S. "Sensation Seeking." http://www.psych.ucsb.edu/ ~kopeikin/sssinfo.htm.

Kristof, Nicholas D. "Our Basic Human Pleasures: Food, Sex and Giving," New York Times Op-Ed, January 16, 2010.

Kroll, Andy. "The New American Oligarchy." Truthout, December 2, 2010.

Krugman, Paul. "The Great Illusion," New York Times Op-Ed, August 8, 2008.

Krugman, Paul. "The Big Zero." New York Times Op-Ed, December 27, 2009.

Krugman, Paul. "Rule by Rentiers." New York Times Op-Ed, June 10, 2011.

Krugman, Paul. "The Centrist Cop-Out." New York Times Op-Ed, July 28, 2011.

Krugman, Paul. "Republicans Against Science." New York Times Op-Ed, August 28, 2011.

Krugman, Paul. "The Fatal Distraction." New York Times Op-Ed, September 4. 2011.

Krugman, Paul. "Free To Die." New York Times Op-Ed, September 15, 2011.

Kuhn, Thomas. (1962). The Structure of Scientific Revolutions. Univ. of Chicago Press.

Leiserowitz, Anthony A., Kates, Robert W. & Parris, Thomas M. "Sustainability Values, Attitudes, and Behaviors: A Review of Multinational and Global Trends. Annu. Rev. Environ. Resour. 2006. 31:413-44.

Leiserowitz, Anthony A. & Fernandez, Lisa O. (Forward by James Gustave Speth and Afterword by Stephen R. Kellert.) Report stemming from: "Toward a New Consciousness: Values to Sustain Human and Natural Communities," a conference chaired by the Yale School of Forestry and Environmental Studies in Aspen, CO, October 11-14, 2007. Copies freely available at www.yale.edu/environment/publications.

Leonhardt, David. "What Makes People Give?" New York Times, March 9, 2008.

Levitt, Steven D. & Dubner, Stephen J. (2005). Freakonomics: A Rogue Economist Explores the Hidden Side of Everything. William Morrow/HarperCollins.

Levitt, Steven D. & Dubner, Stephen J. (2009). Superfreakonomics: Global Cooling, Patriotic Prostitutes, and Why Suicide Bombers Should Buy Life Insurance. William Morrow/HarperCollins, 2009.

Lichtenberg, Judith. "Is Pure Altruism Possible?" New York Times Opinionator, October 19, 2010.

Lofgren, Mike. "Goodbye to All That: Reflections of a GOP Operative Who Left the Cult." Truthout, September 3, 2011.

Mayer, Jane. "State for Sale." The New Yorker, October 10, 2011. Also listen to "The Multimillionaire Helping Republicans to Win N.C." An interview with Jane Mayer on "Fresh Air with Terry Gross," broadcast on NPR, October 6, 2011.

"New York Takes Up Fracking Issue." Story broadcast on National Public Radio, November 3, 2011 on "Morning Edition." Host Steve Inskeep, reported by David Chanatry.

Nocera, Joe. "Who Could Blame G.E.?" New York Times Op-Ed, April 4, 2011.

Nocera, Joe. "The Last Moderate." New York Times Op-Ed, September 5, 2011.

Norenzayan, Ara & Shariff, Azim F. "The Origin and Evolution of Religious Prosociality," Science, Vol. 322, October 3, 2008, p. 58.

Parker-Pope, Tara. "The Happy Marriage is the 'Me' Marriage." New York Times, December 31, 2010.

Pronin, Emily, et. al. "How We See Ourselves and How We See Others," Science, vol. 320, p. 1177-1180 (5/302008).

Raff, Adam. "Search, but You May Not Find." New York Times Op-Ed, December 27, 2009.

Rampell, Catherine. "Lax Oversight Caused Crisis, Bernanke Says." New York Times, January 4, 2009.

Reich, Robert. "The Zero Economy." Truthout, September 4, 2011 and Reich's blog: http://robertreich.org/post/9709926186.

Rich, Frank. "Truthiness Stages a Comeback," New York Times Week In Review, 9/21/2008, p. 9.

Rich, Frank. "Still the Best Congress Money Can Buy." New York Times Op-Ed, November 27, 2010.

Rutenberg, Jim. "Pro-Republican Groups Prepare Big Push at End of Races." New York Times, October 24, 2010, p.1.

Schmitt, Eric and Lipton, Eric. "Focus on Internet Imams as Al Qaeda Recruiters." New York Times, December 31, 2009.

Schumpeter, Joseph. (1942). Capitalism, Socialism and Democracy.

Simon, Herbert. (1957) Models of Man, Social and Rational: Mathematical Essays on Rational Human Behavior in a Social Setting. New York: Wiley.

Spokane Skeptic. "The Low-Information Voter." August 31, 2009. http://spokaneskeptic.blogspot.com/2009/08/low-information-voters.html

"Secret Money in Iowa." New York Times Editorial, October 26, 2010.

Seife, Charles. (2010). Proofiness: The Dark Arts of Mathematical Deception. Viking.

Shinkle, Kirk. "Is America Losing Its Edge: Giving up on high-tech manufacturing could stifle innovation," interview with Richard Elkus, U.S. News & World Report, 8/18/2008, p. 56.

Shulman,, Seth. (2008) Undermining Science: Suppression and Distortion in the Bush Administration. University of California Press.

Stewart, James B. "Lots of Vitriol for Fed Chief, Despite Facts." New York Times, Business, September 2, 2011.

"The Telltale Wombs of Lewiston, Maine." Story broadcast on National Public Radio, October 8, 2009 on "All Things Considered." Hosts Melissa Block and Michele Norris, interviewer Alix Spiegel.

Thompson, Nicholas. New York Times Book Review, November 8, 2009.

Uchitelle, Louis. "G.D.P. ≠ Happiness: Hey, Big Number, Make Room for the Rest of Us," New York Times Week in Review, 8/31/2008, p. 3.

Vedantam, Shankar. "If It Feels Good To Be Good, It Might Be Only Natural." Washington Post, May 28, 2007.

Wade, Nicholas. "Evolution of the God Gene." New York Times, November 15, 2009.

Wade, Nicholas. "We May Be Born With An Urge To Help." New York Times, November 30, 2009.

Warshauer, Matthew. "Who Wants To Be A Millionaire: Changing conceptions of the American Dream." American Studies Today Online, posted 2/13/2003. http://74.125.95.132/search?q=cache:29bkgeca2mgJ:www.americansc.org.uk/online/American_Dream.htm+%22american+dream%22&cd=3&hl=en&ct=clnk&gl=us&client=safari

Weber, Max. (2002) The Protestant Ethic and The Spirit of Capitalism.
    Penguin Books; translated by Peter Baehr and Gordon C.
    Wells.

Zuckerman, Marv. (1983)   Biological Bases of Sensation Seeking,
    Impulsivity and Anxiety. Erlbaum.

www.ingramcontent.com/pod-product-compliance
Lightning Source LLC
Chambersburg PA
CBHW031924190326
41519CB00007B/404